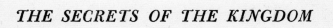

THE SECRETS OF THE KINGDOM

The Secrets
of the Kingdom

By GEORGE JOHNSTON

Illustrations by Charles E. Hewins

The Westminster Press

PHILADELPHIA

Library of Congress Catalog Card No.: 54-7083

Printed in the United States of America
at The Lakeside Press
R. R. Donnelley & Sons Company, Chicago
and Crawfordsville, Indiana

Preface

IN THIS BOOK *I have tried to tell anew the story that is contained in the New Testament. The first part tells of the coming of the Lord Jesus Christ; how he proclaimed to the people of Palestine the good news of God's Kingdom, what perils and adventures he had, how he was betrayed and deserted to suffer the bitter passion of the cross, and at last was gloriously raised from the dead.*

The second part tells how, through the Holy Spirit and the chosen apostles, Christ continued to bring men, women, and children into the family of his Heavenly Father, and under his sovereign rule.

This is the most important story in all the world, and my aim has been to make it come alive for those who read. It is known to us first of all through the New Testament documents, written by apostles and others. These books were written in Greek, and sometimes I have translated passages for myself. Elsewhere I have been glad to use the familiar English translations; or else, to bring out the meaning more clearly, I have paraphrased Scriptures, putting the thoughts more freely into other words. To tell the story as I understand it, I have here and there had to suggest what probably happened, even though we do not know all the facts in detail. But I hope that my readers will want to return from this book to the New Testament itself. To help them to do so there is an index of quotations and references at the back. Using this, they can test for themselves whether I have rightly interpreted the Scriptures. In the latter part of the narrative I have drawn on certain early books of the Church, not found in the Bible, but full of useful information.

Some readers will notice that the order of events in the first part of this book is somewhat different from other accounts of our Lord's life. No one can know precisely under what circumstances every word of Jesus was spoken or every action of his took place; for the four Gospels themselves do not put all the events in the same order. This is because the Gospel writers were not trying to give us a straight or "scientific" biography of Jesus. Apparently Matthew and Luke took Mark's Gospel as a basis of their work, and added stories and sayings of Jesus that they knew from other sources. They did not always keep Mark's order; and John told the life of Jesus in another way again. They were not concerned to give exact details and verbatim reports. They wanted to make clear who and what Jesus Christ is. That must be the aim of every interpreter, with the hope that, through hearing the story told in a fresh way, others will be helped to see in this life the likeness and purpose of God himself.

The secret of the divine Kingdom of love lies in the person and work of Jesus the Nazarene, the Christ of the Jews and Lord of all the nations; to whom therefore, with the Father and the Holy Spirit in the unity of the Godhead, be all glory and honor forever and ever.

GEORGE JOHNSTON.

Contents

PART
I

Looking for a King

1   ON THIS fine spring day Nazareth, lying in the hills of Galilee, was as lovely a village as any round about. The singing of birds, the fresh appearing of the anemones and other flowers, the warm sunshine: everything combined to give one's heart a lift and make one glad to be alive.

The boys hurrying out to school felt the goodness of the morning, and here and there a laggard loitered on the way, unwilling to take up lessons on such a day. But duty prevailed, and they all gathered in the synagogue which was the house of prayer on Sabbaths and their schoolroom on weekdays. Here the local rabbi taught them what God had done for the nation of Israel in years past; how he had made an agreement with them to lead and guard them, on condition that they kept his commandments. Every Jewish boy knew something of the story: the people had been unfaithful, they had forsaken the worship of the one true God and served the idols of their pagan neighbors. God had sent prophet after prophet to preach to them that they must return in repentance to God, else they would lose their liberty. Elijah, Isaiah, Amos, and Jeremiah were the names of some of these prophets. Their word had come true. Now Israel was no longer a free nation. The Romans occupied the land, and before them Syrians and Egyptians had fought for the mastery in Palestine. Samaria had been settled with foreigners; Jerusalem, their glorious capital and holy city, had been pillaged and destroyed.

Ah, but once they had had kings of their own! Saul was the first—Saul the giant who fell in battle along with his greathearted son Jonathan at Gilboa; you could see Gilboa from the hills above Nazareth. Even before that tragic episode God had chosen a young man not of Saul's family at all to be his successor. Men told how the wise priest and judge called Samuel had been sent to Bethlehem to choose and anoint the shepherd lad David as the future king of Israel. Round their campfires they told many tales of the valor of David and the glory he had won in countless exploits against the Philistines. David it was who had made Jerusalem, the city of Zion, his capital; David had been "the sweet singer of Israel," and everyone sang his songs and psalms. Yes, they were great days long ago when Israel had a king; if only they had a king now!

This day the teacher told them a moving story about one of the prophets and one of the kings many years after the time of David. This is the story:

"In the days of Ahab, king in Samaria, there was a vineyard next to the royal palace in the small town of Jezreel. It was owned by a certain Naboth. Ahab saw how well kept and how fertile it was, and he coveted it for himself.

" 'Give me your vineyard, Naboth,' he said, 'for I want to make it into a vegetable garden. In exchange you can have all the money you want or another portion of land.'

" 'O my lord and king, I cannot do that,' replied Naboth without a moment's hesitation. 'This is the land to which I fell heir; all my fathers lived and worked here before me and I could not be loyal to their trust if I gave it away, even to my lord the king. I pray you to excuse me.'

"Upon hearing this, Ahab went off in a sulky temper. When he got home he stayed in his room and refused to eat. Naturally this came to the ears of his queen, Jezebel, and she came to see what was troubling him. Ahab told her what had happened.

" 'What insolence!' exclaimed the proud queen. 'This is not the way kings and their subjects behave in my native land of Syria, and this is not how they should act in the land of Israel. You must not tolerate such stubbornness. Are not you the king? Just you wait, my lord Ahab, there are ways and means to deal with men like this traitor Naboth! Leave it to me.'

"So Ahab gave Jezebel a free hand, and the crafty queen wrote letters, sealed with Ahab's great seal and sent in his name, to the headmen and freemen of Jezreel, outlining the plan: 'You shall assemble a crowd of the townspeople and arrange false accusations to be made against Naboth.'

"Everything fell out as Jezebel had commanded. Naboth was accused of blasphemy against God and treason against the king. They hustled him outside the town limits at once and there stoned him to death. Next day, after the news had reached her, the queen came into Ahab's presence and saluted him joyfully: 'Rise, my lord, O king! Are you not king in Samaria and in Israel? Go now, for all is accomplished and the vineyard you desire in Jezreel is yours. Naboth the traitor is dead!'

"Ahab listened to her word and did what she told him.

"But neither of them reckoned with Elijah, the prophet of God Most High. As soon as Elijah heard the story of the murder, he lifted up his heart to God in prayer, and the word of God sounded in his ears. Immediately he sought out the king.

" 'Listen to me, Ahab! This is the word of the Lord our God: "Where dogs licked up the blood of Naboth, there shall dogs lick up your blood, and your dynasty shall be ruined." '

"Ahab was religious enough to be terrified by these awful words of judgment; in the manner of those days he tore his clothes and put on sackcloth of mourning. And again the word came to Elijah and this time it spared Ahab because of his repentance. 'Nevertheless,' said God, 'your dynasty shall fall to ruin in the reign of your son.' And so it proved."

Late in the afternoon of that day, when school was over, the boy Jesus of Nazareth received permission from his mother, Mary, to climb the hills above the village. He liked to go up there and gaze out over the wide Plain of Esdraelon. After he heard the history of far-off days he found that this plain took on fresh meaning. Yonder lay Gilboa, and one could well imagine the armies of Israel fighting against the Philistines. On a clear day like this he could just see Mt. Carmel in the distance and it reminded him again of the prophet Elijah; for on that hill Elijah had won a dramatic victory over the pagan priests of the native gods.

Thinking of those days and of the present, when Jews groaned under the heel of their enemies, the boy began to recall the things that people, fearful of the Roman overlords, whispered among themselves. Once they had had kings of their own, and their holy Scriptures told them that their God was forever their rightful King. He had promised that he would keep faith with them always; he had raised up mighty leaders in other generations; there was a much cherished hope that one day the dynasty of King David might once again sit on the throne. When would God act to change the present state of affairs? When would he intervene to save them? When would he send another prophet to teach and inspire the nation?

Some people said that it was impossible for the longed-for deliverance to come until Elijah in some mysterious way came back to Israel. God must raise up another prophet who would speak and act with the courage Elijah had shown toward Ahab. Things were bad enough; surely then the time for God to act could not be far away? It was common knowledge that some of the wealthy leaders in Jerusalem were quite content to let the Romans rule. There was a king of sorts in Galilee who owed his power to the favor of the enemy; this was Herod, son of Herod the Great. But Herod was only half a Jew and he was not a very good man, so there was no chance of his being the chosen leader God would send.

The people were looking for a king still; they called him Messiah, the Anointed of the Lord; but no one really knew what kind of person this Messiah might be, and different parties in the nation had their own ideas about the kind they wanted.

Jesus himself was a boy who thought more about God than about a new kingdom in the land. He felt specially close in spirit to God in heaven; he called him *Abba,* meaning Father, and constantly talked with him in prayer. Jesus believed that his Father was the Lord of all the world out there. He had created the heavens and the earth; he made the grass to grow and the spring flowers to bloom; he watched over the stars and the moon, high and lifted up in the glory of the sky. What limits could there be to his power? Southward there lay Samaria, where once Ahab ruled: it was God's. Farther south, beyond the range of sight, lay Judea and on its hill was Jerusalem, the city of David: it was God's. Eastward were the deserts on the other side of the River Jordan and in Syria: was it not all God's? But there was still no limit to the range of Jesus' imagination as he looked out across Esdraelon. He knew that below Carmel was the Great Sea round which were scattered many lands: Italy, from which the Romans had come, Greece, Egypt, and Gaul. Tales had reached him of lands yet farther to the west that lay in the legendary ocean, distant Britain and Thule on the rim of the world: all these lands, he said to himself, are God's! And far, far to the east here were lands to which brave men might venture in caravan after they crossed Esdraelon—India, Persia, Babylon, and Arabia. He knew very little about them, but he did know that the Jews had been scattered by their enemies over the face of the earth, and therefore God must reign there too. From his vantage point in the hills above Nazareth they seemed to lie spread out before his vision: all the kingdoms of this world! And Jesus too, like the others in his nation, was waiting for the day when God would let the world know that he was King in fact and that he was going to rescue and restore his people Israel. When, oh, when, would that day come?

Night came on quickly and he could see the flicker of the lamps in the houses below as he descended to his home once more.

One day Jesus heard with great excitement that he was

to go with his parents to Jerusalem, the Holy City and the capital of the nation. He was going to see the city of King David! He would worship there in the magnificent new Temple that Herod the Great had started to build. This Temple was the focus for all Israel and for all dispersed Jews; here the priests in colorful ritual performed the sacrifices to God, and here once every year the high priest entered the Holy of Holies to make atonement for the sins of the nation during the year that had passed. In Jerusalem, perhaps Jesus would hear news of what was going on among the other nations of the world and perhaps whether the leaders of the Jews there were expecting anything to happen soon. He was twelve years old and himself almost ready to play a man's part.

Jerusalem proved every bit as exciting as he had hoped, but for his parents the visit provided a moment of dreadful anxiety and of new insight into the heart of their boy. When the caravan started back for home, Jesus was not with Mary or Joseph; they assumed that he would be with other friends from Galilee. Then they discovered that he was not in the caravan at all! Off they hurried in some alarm to the city, searching for him here, there, and everywhere, till at last, to their great relief, they came on him in the courts of the Temple. He was listening to the rabbis, the teachers of the laws of God and interpreters of religious traditions; and not only listening, for he answered their questions to him and in turn put deep questions to them. Teachers and parents alike were astonished when they saw the wisdom and devotion to God that he showed. Distracted and concerned, however, Mary broke in on the scene, saying: "Why have you done this to us, child? Your father and I have been looking for you everywhere in sorrow. We were afraid that something had happened to you." Jesus looked at her lovingly. "Did you search for me so anxiously, Mother? I am sorry that I caused you this fear. Did it not occur to you that I would be in my Father's house?"

Then they left Jerusalem and set off for Nazareth, where they had to tell the whole story of their stay to James and Jude, the younger brothers in the family, and to other families in the village who had never gone on a pilgrimage to the capital.

Jesus grew to manhood in Nazareth and stayed there till he was nearly thirty years of age. It is probable that Joseph died during this time, while the other children were quite young, so that Jesus had to carry the burdens of head of the family. He was the village carpenter, and there was always plenty of work to be done for the villagers and the farmers of the countryside.

Like any mother, Mary had her own work too: sweeping out the house, baking the bread, patching the clothes, nursing those who fell sick, helping neighbors, and showing kindness to the poor and aged. From her the children had first learned the name of God in heaven; with her they sang the songs of the faith; and by her knee they heard stories from the Scriptures. She taught them to be obedient to their parents and respectful to older men and women, to say grace at table in gratitude for the daily mercies of God, and to repeat at bedtime the evening prayer, "Father, into thy hands I commend my spirit."

Jesus, conscious of a special sense of being God's son and God's servant, spent much time in prayer with his Heavenly Father. He attended diligently the services in the synagogue and became deeply learned in the whole Bible: the laws given through Moses, the prophecies, and the psalms. Jesus learned the ancient Hebrew language in which the Scriptures had been written and judged for himself the traditional interpretations handed on from rabbi to rabbi. No one was more highly regarded for his religious devotion and his loving spirit than Jesus of Nazareth, the son of Mary.

He knew very well, however, that it was not every home that gave its children such an example of simple goodness and honest work as his own had given to him. In the neighboring villages, Nain and Cana, and farther away beside the Lake of Galilee, at Capernaum and Bethsaida, there were many people to whom the divine laws did not matter very much. Some Jewish families there had intermarried with unbelieving foreigners, contrary to the custom of the nation, and the region was scornfully called "Galilee of the Gentiles."

Farmers and laborers who came into the carpenter's shop sometimes talked about the difficult times, the high prices of foodstuffs, the heavy taxes of Herod. "Down yonder in Bethsaida," said John Bar-Simeon, "there is a wicked judge who takes bribes from the wealthy and is not interested in giving justice. I am told that the widow of Joshua Bar-Jacob simply can't get him to grant her an interview to state her case."

"It's an evil time we are living in," said his neighbor, "when some of these wealthy landowners round about here won't pay a man a decent wage. What with taxes for Herod and the tax for the priests of the Temple in Jerusalem and customs duties on the fish out of the lake, it is money out of your pocket all the time. Is it any wonder that the hot-blooded are ganging up to kill Roman soldiers, and the young men are falling into evil ways?"

Jesus knew that much of what they said was exaggerated grumbling, but much of it was true. There were homes in Galilee where children were neglected or beaten; homes where men wasted the family income on luxuries they could not afford. Some wicked people reminded one of Ahab and Jezebel. It was impossible to shut one's eyes to the facts. They were all looking for a king, but many were not eager that a just and loving God should reign over them.

On the other hand, there were humble, God-fearing men and women who did their best to conform to God's will. They tried to obey the counsels of the prophet Micah, "to do justly, and to love mercy, and to walk humbly" with their God. Among such people there was the same national hope, the same intense longing that by mighty acts of God Israel should be set free; but they felt that first the whole nation would have to turn in penitence and trust to God. How could an ungodly nation expect the favor of God? Perhaps if Israel made a very special effort, it could hasten the day of deliverance. Perhaps it would be enough for them to keep the Commandments; or even one of the Commandments! "If only Israel would observe Sabbath perfectly, just for a single day," they sighed, "surely God would descend then and deliver us!"

But for Jesus the important thing was that men and women should live for God by listening to his word. The whole duty of man was obedience to the great laws of love that were to be found in the Scriptures, the laws that were the mainspring of his own life:

Thou shalt love the Lord thy God with all thy heart,
    and with all thy strength and with all thy soul.
Thou shalt love thy neighbor as thyself.

Day after day, whatever his work and whatever was happening in the world and the nation, Jesus of Nazareth took time to be alone with God and to offer his daily prayer:

"Father,
    May thy name be sanctified,
    May thy kingdom come,
    May thy will be done:
    as in heaven, so in earth."

The day when he saw that Kingdom come with power would mark the end of an age, perhaps the end of the world as he knew it. The time and the season of that only God knew, for all times were in his hand. It would come! The hand of God was still effective and his arm was not shortened that it could not save! But the sign—what would be the sign of its coming? Was it true that God would first send "another Elijah"?

One day when he was about thirty years of age Jesus received news that made him wonder if the hour had struck at last.

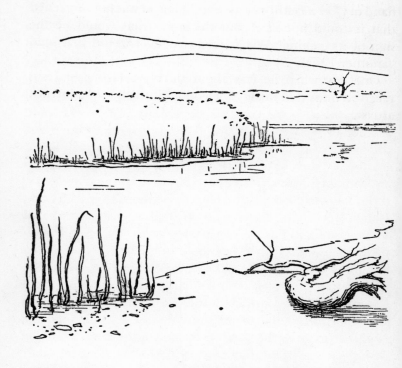

The Last of the Prophets

2 A GREAT and unusual excitement had begun to stir among the inhabitants of Jerusalem and Judea. Priests whispered to each other in the Temple, "Have you heard what John the son of Zachariah is up to?" Rabbis spoke about the reports that kept arriving telling of the new preacher John who stood by the banks of the Jordan and called all true Jews to repent and be baptized. Crowds of

people rushed to the ford in the river to see and hear for themselves, and the one verdict they all reached seemed to be this: "Here is a live, new prophet of God!"

Until this time a prophet was pretty much a figure in the sacred Scriptures, the kind of man God might have raised up in days long, long ago: yet here was one right at one's own doorstep! There had been plenty of priests all through the years, for the work of the national religion demanded them; and in any event only the children of priests could succeed to the priesthood. This kind of religious man was different; no one took upon himself the office of a prophet, because, as men said with wonder in their hearts, prophets appear only when God himself makes it possible. Now, those who had heard all their lives about Amos, Micah, Isaiah, Jeremiah, those who thrilled to the exploits of Elijah, suddenly were confronted with the fact that a preacher like those men was there in the flesh! He spoke in the grand tradition. He talked with the freedom of a man who had received his commission, not from other teachers, but directly from God. He was like an Amos, a Micah, and an Elijah all rolled into one individual. Look at his strange clothing, exactly the sort of thing a wild man from the desert, such as Elijah had been, would wear: a camel's hair cloak that would keep out the tearing, driving winds of the wilderness and the blinding fury of the sandstorms. This John, too, had been content to live for weeks alone among the rocks, sometimes fasting for days, sometimes eating wild honey or whatever fat, juicy insects he could find.

John's father, Zachariah, was a country priest and that meant that for one week in the year he would go up to the Temple in Jerusalem and help to perform the ritual. This was a high honor and privilege, for through the worship of the Temple the Jews received encouragement and direction for their lives. They believed that the prayers and sacrifices brought the nation into genuine fellowship with God, their sins were forgiven, their daily work was consecrated. So Zachariah and his wife, Elizabeth, were specially glad when, late in their lives, a baby son was born to them; one day he too would carry on the priestly line. But the young man John had left all this behind and gone off to the lonely and forbidding wilderness of Judea.

The priests in Jerusalem were very important leaders in the political life of the country, but many of them were suspected of being overfriendly with the Roman officials and too willing to compromise the Jewish way of life. The aristocrats among them were called the Sadducees. But John was of a different stamp. He was a dreamer and a man of strong moral convictions; he would never be a priest in that crowd! He would leave the intrigues and the glories of the capital to seek among the dreary rocks of the desert God's will for his life. And there he found it. John, the son of Zachariah the priest, came from the desert as a prophet of the Lord with his, "This is the word of God." Like great preachers before him he had had a vision of the Lord high and lifted up, and in obedience to the call he had heard had begun by the Jordan River to declare his message.

A real live prophet! God at work among his people! After many years the miracle had happened again. Rabbis might claim to have the divine Spirit to teach them, yet no rabbi had dared to preach with the freedom and power of this dynamic man from the desert. What could this mean? Was God about to act and bring in the Kingdom?

The strangeness of the event lay not merely in the man's distinctive clothing nor in his prophetic message. John spoke to the people as those who had sinned against God and who had failed in the special purpose for which God had chosen them. He demanded that those who were moved by his preaching should do something definite about it: they must enter the waters of the River Jordan and accept baptism for the forgiveness of their sins. Other teachers required converts to the Jewish religion from other nations to take baptism; John said the Jews themselves needed it. God would be content with nothing else!

"Who are you?" men would ask him.

"After me there is coming One who is stronger than I am," he would tell them. "I am not worthy to be the servant who will loosen the thong of his sandals and wait upon him. I am simply one who has been called to prepare the way for his arrival."

"When will this Other you speak of appear?"

To this question the preacher could not give any definite reply. There was mystery that he knew not of; one thing he was glad to say: his own business was to help the nation to make ready for the crisis of the coming. And when they asked him what sort of work that Other would do, John's eyes flashed and his voice in answer was terrible as the tramp of an army marching with all the weapons of war. He sounded like a thoroughly roused and passionate crusader against corruption in high places:

"The Strong One will do God's strange work among you; he will bring to completion what is already going on, for even now God is at work in your midst."

Down the valley of the Jordan echoed with ominous ring his tremendous cry to his audience: "Repent! Repent! Flee from the wrath to come! At this very moment the ax has been laid to the roots of the trees and all the fruitless ones will come crashing down, fit only for the fire. Save yourselves; come to these waters of Jordan, where of old others came and were made clean in body and spirit. Except you repent of lust and cruelty, you will perish; you must confess before Almighty God that you have broken his laws and forfeited his favor. Soon! only do it soon, for the Strong One coming after me comes quickly. I can almost feel his hot breath upon me. Beware of his harvest, for the breath of his mouth will sweep away the useless chaff into the endless fires of hell!

"I baptize you with water;
   he will baptize you with his Breath. . . .
I offer you now, before he comes, a way of escape:
   he will carry the pruning knife and the winnowing
      fork. . . .

I can promise you forgiveness now, and salvation hereafter, if you come to the baptism of repentance. He will suddenly appear: where? in the Temple? in the land of Israel? No man knows the place of his visitation. Is it not written in Malachi the prophet: 'And the Lord, whom you seek, will suddenly come to his temple, even the messenger of the covenant. . . . But who may abide the day of his coming? and who shall stand when he appears? For he is like a refiner's fire. . . .' "

Some in the crowds that flocked to Jordan from Jerusalem, from Judea, and even from Galilee and the north would challenge the prophet to give them direct guidance about their own occupations. For example, there were men who had taken the wages of the Roman Empire and now tried to enrich themselves at the expense of their fellow Jews.

"How may we qualify for the new age that is to come?" one of them might ask, rather timidly, for everyone loathed these tax collectors.

"Collect only your dues," was the reply.

Some soldiers cried out, "And we?"

"Take your pay," said John; "you have contracted to serve in the army; be content with what it gives you. Lay hands violently on no man; do not steal, or hurt civilians,

just because you are in uniform; make no false accusations
but let decent folk live in peace."

Represented in the congregation at the river were priests
from Jerusalem, who ventured to suggest that they might
have a place in the new order. But at this John bristled in
bitter anger:

"You!" he cried to them. Scornfully he looked them over
and went on: "You! Brood of serpents that you are! Who
warned *you* to flee from the wrath to come?"

And there were others who questioned him. They were
Jews who were very conscious of being a chosen people, the
children of Abraham, the nation of God's covenant made
ages before with Abraham, then with Jacob and with Moses.
Every week these men and women heard in the synagogue
the sacred Book of the Covenant in which Moses and the
prophets declared the will and the word of God. Surely
the Strong One, that mysterious figure of whom this new
prophet talked, must be in some way their God's appointed
leader and deliverer! And did not any Jew, just because he
was a Jew, have a *right* to share in the pleasures and blessings
of the new age when it came? With thoughts like these in
their heads, they opened their mouths to ask John what he
believed. John had seen through their pretense and their
pride. Not all the words that he spoke were written down,
but it is easy to imagine what he must have said:

"You think that you deserve to escape condemnation
when He comes; but I tell you that much shall be required of you. You are Jews who pride yourselves on
having a special place in the plans of God. I bid you not
to despise these tax collectors and these soldiers: are
you really any better in God's sight than they? If you
presume to call yourselves the people of God, you must
begin to practice charity and brotherliness. For the
Lord our God has told you in the prophecies that he

prefers to see the naked clothed and the hungry fed than a lot of pilgrims in the Temple sight-seeing and enjoying themselves or a crowd at the synagogue whose chief concern is the size of their profit on market day, whose worst fault is cheating and exploiting their fellow Jews. Will you dare to claim Abraham as your 'father'? Then you must render to God the same sort of trust and obedience that Abraham gave. You know the story. Abraham was certain that he had heard the call of God and he set forth on his travels. He was actually willing to offer up his son in sacrifice and he never had any doubt that God would fulfill his covenant promises. But in our generation we Jews have not been obedient, so, unless we repent, the coming of a new servant of God will prove to be our undoing. Israel the holy nation must turn again to its God. I tell you, out of these very stones the God of Abraham, the God of the miracle that brought Isaac to birth, the God of my father Zachariah, can raise up new children for Abraham, to take our place."

John's words did not fall entirely on deaf ears. Many went down into the water of Jordan and confessed their sins. Some men attached themselves to John as his disciples, among them some Galileans from Bethsaida and Capernaum, fishing centers on the Lake of Galilee. They and their friends carried the news of the new preacher and the new baptism up and down the country. Herod heard about him and wondered what this would lead to; the Romans, of course, knew everything that was going on, but they could hardly be expected to assess the significance of the movement. In the Temple the high priest and his chief associates discussed the message of this country priest's son and were baffled by it. Rumors were current among some of the more enthusiastic followers of John that he himself might be the

Messiah, who was simply waiting for the time when he could proclaim himself openly.

There could be no question that John the Baptizer, as they called him, had stirred up the national life and religion as had no one before him for centuries. Men recalled how nearly two hundred years ago other leaders had arisen, how they had led the Jewish army to battle after battle until they had founded an independent kingdom—but that was such a long time ago! If only God would give them a new leader and a new kingdom! If only they could get rid of the Romans and the half-Jewish house of Herod, and establish a kingdom in true succession to David!

Others pointed out that this John gave no indication that he would or could lead an army. His talk was religious and moral. He insisted on purity. He attacked even the priests of God. Courage he had, but what sort of courage was any good that did not promise liberation from the enemy? Nevertheless John was a portent of something or Someone; and the hearts of many were roused to great dreams and hopes.

John himself said nothing further about the Kingdom of the Lord or about the Messiah. Over and over again he kept repeating that he was simply a voice; that through him God was speaking to the nation and summoning them to be ready by repenting. Wherever he moved in the valley of the Jordan, in and out of the territory of King Herod, John cried out in warning and encouragement. His words terrified the weakhearted and the sinful who realized their unfaithfulness, yet to many they brought decision and commitment because they wanted release from evil habits and ungodly ways.

"Repent," cried the voice of John, "repent, all you Jews, and all you outcasts and strangers! Even at this moment the processes of divine judgment are going on. Soon there will come after me a Stronger One. I am just a voice crying in this desert. I am only the herald of his approach. With the hot breath of his mouth he will destroy the wicked. But if you repent and get baptized, you may escape his anger. Come therefore, come at once, come soon to the baptism of repentance and the forgiveness of sins; come now, now, before it is too late—now, lest he come so suddenly that you are taken unawares and you perish!"

The Call of Jesus

3 IN NAZARETH the carpenter Jesus was busy in his workshop, for his family was poor and there was much to be done. People knew him as one of the kindest and most devout men ever known in that village. They went to him with their troubles and found comfort in his sympathy and understanding. Jesus helped them to believe that God cared for them and was to be trusted. Boys and girls ran

about his yard and loved to listen to his stories; he gave them much of his time and always entered into their fun. When there was death or sickness in Nazareth, Jesus was close to the troubled, full of concern and helpfulness. It was as if all the joys and sorrows of the villagers were his own. He understood the burdens of poverty and the longing for freedom that good Jews cherished. He had seen soldiers beat men and frighten women for no apparent reason, except that they liked to show off and to use their strength. Jesus knew also how many Jews hated not only the Roman masters but their own Jewish landlords; how some were thieves, cheats, and bullies. All this grieved him deeply, for he looked on the Jewish people as those whom God the Father had chosen to be his servants. They all belonged together and he himself belonged with them as with a single family. So he felt the disgrace of it, the shame of it, the ungodliness of it, that this people should sin against God by cutting one another's throats.

Jesus was aware too that God his Father had service for him to perform, at present in his shop, but later perhaps in other places. One day he might see the Kingdom of his Father set up in the land and all the kingdoms of this world brought to the Father's allegiance. Meantime he waited in Nazareth, ever devoted to the religion of his Father's house, constant in his attendance at the synagogue, learned in the Scriptures, a holy, loving, gracious man, the Son of the Father.

And now to Nazareth as well as to Capernaum and Bethsaida had come the word of John the Baptist's mission to Israel. Jesus heard enough: "After me is coming Another . . . . Prepare for the new age . . . . Live a new life, all of you," to realize that this was the sign he had been waiting for! The Judge who was to come and sweep away injustice, to restore the national piety, must be God's agent for the establishment of his Kingdom. This was the beginning of a new era and John was its sign! God had raised up at last a new prophet, a man of the word. This was God's doing and it was wonderful in the eyes of men. This was another Elijah, called by God to rebuke the leaders and the people of Israel so that they might learn to serve God in righteousness. And if John was the other Elijah the Jews expected, . . . if that Other he was said to talk about was therefore the Messiah of the Lord, . . . and if the Father had special work for Jesus to do, then this was the hour for decision. He must leave Nazareth at once and proceed to the Jordan. He must go on pilgrimage to see this sign that had come to pass. He must go and listen to this prophet of God through whom God might say something of decisive importance to himself.

With mounting excitement Jesus made his plans. The work of the carpenter's shop must be handled by James and Jude. His mother Mary must be assured that he felt called of God thus to leave home for an indefinite period. There was no telling when he would return, for there was as yet no certain word to tell what his future course of action would be. All that he knew was that he must find out for himself what the message of the new prophet was and what this would mean for his own life. Good-by! Good-by! He has gone on pilgrimage to the Jordan, to see John the Baptist, the prophet of God, and to hear his word.

At the river Jesus found that great crowds still came to hear also. They heard terrifying words of judgment on the sins of the nation and the evil of their lives, and some of them were shocked and angered. They heard John bravely condemn the immorality of the court of Herod Antipas, and some whispered that he might pay for such talk with his neck. Jesus heard and agreed that there was much evidence to justify the attacks of John. There were rich men who cared nothing for public opinion or the approval of God. There were pious leaders who drew attention to themselves instead of to God, by making a public exhibition of themselves at street corners, saying long prayers, showing how emaciated they were because of much fasting. These people made a fuss every time they rubbed shoulders with the ordinary man who knew little about ritual washing before meals and cared less; the "religious" felt they had been contaminated by this contact. They had no feeling of brotherhood; they were self-righteous. Jesus had seen them in different towns and in Jerusalem itself. Their very faces gave them away, for they had none of the grace and serenity that religion should bring to the worshipers of God his Father. Jesus agreed with John that all was not well with the morals even of the "good and godly" among the chosen nation, the Jews. So they needed to repent and make a new start; this baptism of John's was just the thing they required. But should Jesus himself accept it?

He listened further to the kind of thing John said in reply to inquirers. Decisively and directly John dealt with the unpopular tax collectors; Jesus thought with a rueful smile of Levi, the local collector of customs at Capernaum: this would have been good for Levi to hear! "Collect only your dues." He found justice in the phrase—for the collectors were notorious robbers—but no hard censorship; nothing, for example, about their giving up a disgraceful employment.

When the dangerous question was put by the soldiers in uniform, "What should we do?", John courageously advised them not to lay violent hands on anyone and not to take advantage of their power to steal, or to beat up civilians. The government could not pretend that this prophet was inciting the troops to revolt or desert; there was no sign of revolution here. Yet John made it quite clear that the army had

no right in the eyes of God to play fast and loose with the
people of an occupied country. Jesus thought over the
political implications of preaching such as this.

How devastatingly John dealt with those Jews who felt
that they had complimentary tickets into the new age!
Coldly he reminded them that God's chosen had to be God's
faithful. At every point John set a barrier against deceit and
self-conceit: a man could not expect to get by on descent
from father Abraham; present privilege was no guarantee
for future glory. Jesus thoroughly approved these warnings
to the complacent.

Others who heard the truth uttered by John were not at
all pleased; they were hurt in their self-esteem, and they
were not above adding slander to their opposition. "This
fellow is 'possessed' by a demon," they said; "he is no
prophet but the agent of the devil." Jesus disagreed with
them entirely. In the message of John he recognized a divine
challenge to evil, corruption, ease, and self-indulgence. God
was seeking a holy nation for his service. What, then, should
Jesus himself do?

John insisted that those who found God's judgments
through his words should come down into the river and
wash themselves symbolically in its waters. Sins must be
cleansed. Moreover, this would put a mark on them to certify that they had freely submitted to God and his holy will.
By this they would be separated in a real way from all those
in their nation who felt no necessity for repentance. Baptism would band them together under a single sign. For they
belonged together as those who awaited the Strong One
whom God would send.

Jesus was deeply moved by all that he had heard and seen.
There could be no doubt now that God had indeed raised
up his servant John to bring a much-needed message that
evil must be abandoned. Perhaps John sounded more ter-

rible than God the Father; perhaps John lacked charm and kindness, speaking forever the language of denunciation and doom; yet Jesus knew that John was saying what had to be said. To the accusations of the reformer he said Amen: the nation did need repentance. To the request that the men and women who had responded to God should join themselves to John and to one another by the rite of baptism Jesus found himself saying Amen: that is right and proper. But in that case should he not himself join the movement? Even though he found no cause in his own life to accuse himself of sin, was he to stand aside from this gathering of God's own? Did not obedience mean for him too that he must get baptized? This would be an act showing Jesus' agreement with John's demand for godly life. At the same time it would identify him with all these penitent folk who had already been baptized. The more he thought of this and the more he sought the counsel of his Father in prayer, the more certain he became. He would go down into the waters; he too would confess as a loyal Jew the sins and shortcomings of his fellow men and he would join himself to their company, bearing their sin and sharing their sorrow; offering himself in this way to God for future service.

So with eager joy Jesus came one day to the river to be baptized by John, and in those waters of cleansing he had a most wonderful experience. There in the place of his humility and brotherly obedience the Spirit of God descended upon Jesus, and the power of the divine Spirit entered him in a fresh way. There in that desert ford, where busy men and travelers passed on their business in this world, Jesus the carpenter knew that the Father was calling him at last to the decisive work of his life. He heard God saying to him: "My Son, my Son! How I have waited too for this hour! The fulfillment of the ages has arrived and out of Israel I call you, my Son. Prophets have come and gone; the new Elijah has preached and baptized to prepare your way. You are he that was to come. You are to be to Israel a Messiah, my anointed Servant. This is the hour, and in you I am well pleased. Now you must set your hands to this work of the Kingdom to which I appoint you."

At once Jesus left the river and the company gathered there; in the leading of the Spirit, without faltering or looking back, he walked into the desert places to be alone with God and to consider his mission. For more than a month he stayed in retirement, praying and fasting, absorbed day by day in the contemplation of the Father and this unique vocation to which he must now give himself entirely.

To be a Messiah for Israel! So many men would think that this meant girding himself in royal power, commanding an army of patriots and rising in the wrath of God against the oppressors. They wanted to see King David's greater son on the throne of his fathers, but was this what the Son of God should be? John's work had already shown that there was opposition in the land to the prophetic ministry, with its stubborn insistence that character was far more important than birth or rank or worldly glory. If the new Elijah was of this sort, was the anointed leader to be content with less than this? Jesus knew that the Son was bound by his obedience to the Father and the Father's way. Now, in the exaltation of his vision and call he must try to relate his own mission to that of John. The great burden of John's message about the coming leader had been that he would judge the nation: but exactly how was this sifting to take place? How was he to blow away the chaff from the wheat? When John spoke of the hot breath of the Strong One, was he thinking of the same kind of divine power as Jesus did? Was the Spirit of the Father simply an avenging, terrible agency as dreadful as the searing fires that swept the woodlands, or was it gentle and persuasive? When John talked, was he simply using the language of poetry or did he mean in sober prose that the Messiah of God was actually an executioner of the divine anger? Did this fit what Jesus knew in his own experience of the Father's loving care? Of course God was the all-powerful Lord whose will must be done, and in years past the Spirit had driven mighty men to accomplish tremendous feats of valor. But it seemed far better to think with one of the prophets of the divine Spirit as a re-creating breath, a wind of heaven that blew upon the dying and brought new impulses of life and hope.

Day after day in the lonely desert, paying no attention to his own physical needs but concentrating entirely on the vast new adventure opening out before him, Jesus pondered the scope and the methods of his work as the Messiah. His mind dwelt often on the Scriptures that he knew so well; he prayed continuously; he committed his whole personality to the guidance of the Spirit of God.

Yet the more he thought of his lifework, the more he was assailed by opposing ideas; the desert became a battleground, and it seemed that the tired, hungry man had become a prey for the attacks of evil.

First came the suggestion: "You are hungry, feed yourself. If you are really the Son of God, turn these stones into bread! Think what you can do when you leave here in renewed strength. You too can feed the poor and the hungry, the dispossessed, the unfortunate Jews on whom the rising cost of living bears most heavily. Feed them, as God fed them in the wilderness during their escape from Egypt! Feed them in this modern age and show them that a greater than Moses is here! This is the way to prove to them that you are indeed the One they await, for not even God can expect a nation to fight his battles valiantly on an empty stomach."

Oh, it was a plausible idea! He was famished, and many

of his fellows were continually looking to see where the next meal would come from, worried for the sake of their children. They would certainly throng to him if he promised them abundance. But there was that subtle "if"—"if you are the Son of God"—trying to undermine the whole basis of his future. Jesus reacted with vigor against the temptation. "No," he cried, "man must not put bread before God. This is intolerable distrust—to think that God does not know our needs before we ask him or that he will not supply all our wants so long as we give ourselves to his service. It is man's inhumanity, his greed and fear, that prevent everyone from having enough to eat. How dare you suggest that the Messiah should take into his own hands what God has reserved for himself? What devilry is this that would pretend that perhaps, after all, I am not the Messiah-Son of God? I have heard his word! I have answered his call! Let me alone, for I must seek ever to satisfy the deepest needs of my people. For it is written in the Scriptures:

" 'Man shall not live by bread alone,
     but by every word that proceeds
     from the mouth of God.' "

He thought of the holy place in Jerusalem where the nation centered its worship of God; he remembered the bustle of men driving into the courtyards the sacrificial animals, the shouts of pilgrims, the clink of the coins at the exchangers' tables where pilgrims paid their dues in foreign currency. He saw again the solemn rabbis clustered in groups to discuss the weighty matters of the law and heard some of their hairsplitting interpretations. Was this the way men should draw near to the Father? Surely the Messiah would reform and purify the Temple courts?

And then into his mind entered the idea: "Why don't you fly to the holy Temple in Jerusalem? If you are the Son of God, the Messiah, leap from the topmost pinnacle of the

Temple towers and take possession of the national religion.
Then you can do what you like with it! People will acclaim
you. You need have no fear about attempting such a feat; is
it not also in the Scriptures, 'God will give his angels charge
over you; they will bear you up, lest you strike your foot
against a rock'?"

There it was again, that evil proposal to doubt his own
right to be Messiah. But it was surely still more cunning to
make use of Scripture to entrap him! What did this mean?
What possible reason could be given for so fantastic an
attempt to control the national worship of God? "It is pre-
posterous," he cried. "You can't make me try to find out in
this way if I am really God's Messiah. It is written also in
the Scriptures, 'You shall not put the Lord your God to the
test.'"

But now temptation assailed him in another form. He
was attacked again and again; he was made to understand
just how momentous was the task to which he was committed. To be the anointed of God meant that he must do
battle against wickedness in high places. He would be the
leader to set up the Kingdom of God. He must work with
the kind of men and women that were in Israel—priests,
rabbis, counselors, farmers, peasants, good and bad and in-
different. Herod Antipas controlled much of the area. Rome
lorded it over all. Ideas from many quarters flowed into
Palestine and competed for the mastery. How was God's
rule to be established except by conquest? He must learn
to be in some sense the Strong One of whom John the Baptist
had spoken. One man against a multitude. One man against
all the armies of evil powers. One man seeking universal
dominion in the name of the one Lord God.

Now it was as if from a loftier perch than the hills above
Nazareth he looked out over a plain far vaster than the Plain
of Esdraelon. East, west, north, and south, it was as if the

whole earth lay stretched out before him, the Messianic Ruler, the Vicegerent of God. Here was God's rightful possession! To win these he was dedicated.

"Ah, but I can tell you how to do it," whispered the tempter. "I will give you authority over all these kingdoms of this world. It belongs to me and I can give it to anyone I choose. There is only one condition and that is very easy: fall down and do homage for them to me! Other leaders have done this and conquered; let the end justify the means. You have magnificent powers and a wonderful opportunity to do good by winning great glory and power. Fall down!"

"Blasphemy, blasphemy!" replied Jesus. "The prince of evil does not have the final authority in this world. My Father is King. Fool that you are, to offer what is not yours to give! Satan that you are, evil, ungodly, unscrupulous, get you gone from me! I am the King-Messiah because I am my Father's Son, and to me he has given these kingdoms. Not by your way, but by his, shall I conquer. I am his Servant to learn and to obey. He only reigns in glory, and before him only must one fall down and do homage. For it is written, 'You shall worship the Lord your God and him only shall you serve.'"

With this tremendous assertion of his rank and his obedience Jesus routed the tempter for a time. Jesus knew now what he could not do. He knew how dangerous would be his work and how difficult, for he was to bring the love and the goodness of God into the common life of Israel and the world, into the midst of entrenched special interests, into the confusion of a world where many even of the best sought only their own advantage. He had to share with people like that his knowledge of the Father's unwearying patience and his longing that they should live together in peace and charity. He could not go to them as the sort of Messiah they expected, for he was not to be a new and mightier David;

he was not to be a wiser and more imperious Moses. He would not fly down to them from the skies breathing out fire and brimstone, blowing away the weak and the sinful. He was still Jesus of Nazareth; he was a man well known there, the village carpenter, the man learned in the Scriptures and loved for his grace and sympathy. Such a man he must continue to be, the humble Servant of God's will; and yet also the One whom God had chosen, the One in whom and for whom all the resources of heaven were available.

He would go to the nation as a teacher and a preacher. He would seek to bind up the brokenhearted and distressed, he would comfort the mourners and cheer the faint with the news of God's sovereign love. In his own way God would crown his work with success, just as at his own time God would say to him: "The time is up! Begin now! Go forth in my name and teach them the gospel of the Kingdom!" Till then he must leave the wilderness and return to the towns and villages. In Jerusalem and Judea he visited friends and relatives; he talked with many who were eagerly looking for the new age. And as he moved about the country, he watched and waited for the next sign and the next call.

The Hand of Herod
or the Hand of God?

4 OTHERS besides John's followers had taken notice of what was going on at the fords of Jordan.

The rulers of the country had to be on a constant lookout for dangerous movements among the people, for it was well known that there was nothing many Jews would have liked better than the rise of a popular leader. Their nationalism went very deep and their ardor in battle could be absolutely fanatical. What was all the more menacing in their case was the possibility that a leader might emerge who would summon them in the name of their fathers' God. They were the most stiff-necked of religious people. In God's name they were capable of the utmost sacrifices, and the slightest whisper could set their world ablaze. A new David or a new Moses to deliver them out of the hand of their enemies was what they awaited, and they sang spirited songs of faith which promised them that their God was one who kept his promises and would upset the mighty from their seats. Was this perhaps the meaning of this new prophet and baptist, John the son of Zachariah? So in Judea itself, directly under the administration of the Roman province of Syria, the responsible Roman official, Pontius Pilate, posted agents to keep an eye on John's movement.

When John went north into Galilee and Perea, ruled by Herod Antipas, nominally king there by Roman consent, the palace was informed and sent out its own agents to assess the meaning of the new religious leader. Herod was himself part Jew and he was very sensitive to anything that might threaten his royal house. Since any "Coming One" was almost certain to be a menace to his kingdom, careful note had to be taken for seditious talk about a King-Messiah.

Among the reports that were submitted to him Herod found most offensive those that detailed the kind of moral guidance John was giving. Herod had special reason to dislike and to fear a high standard of personal behavior upheld with prophetic fervor and authority. He had married a princess of Arabia, because it behooved him to stay on good terms with his Arab neighbors, but he was in love with another woman. Herod wasted neither words nor time on the matter. He simply brought his beloved home to the palace and enjoyed the pleasures of sin to his heart's content. His wife fled in anger to her father. The other woman was perfectly willing to become the mistress of this king who, to make matters worse, was both her uncle and her brother-in-law. For she was Herodias, the daughter of one half brother of Antipas and the wife of another half brother. And her husband was still alive. All in all, the court scandal was a nasty business. Herodias had a daughter, Salome, of whom Antipas made much when she was brought to his court.

Then came the news that John the Baptist had entered the territories of Herod and was urging vehemently repentance for just those sins to which the king was prone. Herod was enraged. Fox that he was, however, he did not act in haste. John was warned to be careful, and everything might have been well if only John could have realized that kings are above morality. But John thought otherwise and had the courage of his convictions. Like another Elijah, he stormed into the presence of Herod and denounced him: "It is not lawful for you to have this woman." Herod showed not a moment of grief or penitence. Without more ado he threw John into the safe and distant dungeons of his fortress at Machaerus. That would show the world who was king in Galilee and Perea!

"The hand of Herod has been laid on John!" Traders in the bazaars of Jerusalem and Tiberias passed on the news from one to another. The scattered disciples of John spread the news too: "The prophet of God has been silenced in the kingdom of Herod!" Through Judea, Samaria, and Galilee flashed the story: "The hand of Herod has arrested John the Baptist. What will happen next? Where is the promise of the Strong One who is to come?" Many shrugged their shoulders, saying skeptically, "It has all been a false alarm; God has let us down again."

When the news reached Jesus, it moved him profoundly. He could not agree that God had abandoned either his prophet or his people. He remembered how often the prophets of the Lord in days gone by had been stoned, rejected, laughed to scorn, and their words unheeded. But God could not be silenced in this way. God, who can do all that he chooses to do, had allowed this to happen to John because John's work was finished. Other plans were readied and another Servant stood awaiting his summons to action. "This is it!" Jesus said to himself. "This is the sign and the call for which I have been waiting. God be merciful to John and help him in his trials; God be with me now in my mission! The hand of Herod may be able to silence John, but it cannot silence my Heavenly Father."

Immediately Jesus set out for Galilee, the territory of Herod Antipas. To the kingdom of this ungodly ruler Jesus went with word of another Kingdom; to the place where John had given his witness Jesus went with his own message and his own different approach to Israel.

"Good news!" he cried. "Good news!

The time is up and God's hour has struck!

God's sovereign power has begun its final work
   among you.

Turn again to God and listen,

listen to the gospel of God,

for his Kingdom is at your doors!"

He came to Capernaum by the Lake of Galilee and began to preach by the seaside. And crowds flocked to hear this new leader who seemed to have started where John left off. Before long they realized that here too God was speaking to them, that prophecy had not flickered and died with the imprisoned Baptist. So they listened to the simple and homely words of the man from Nazareth:

"What figure shall I use for the Kingdom of God? Or to what shall I compare it?

"It is like a grain of mustard seed, very tiny. A man took

some and planted it in his plot; and lo! the seed grew till it became a tree. The birds of the sky nested in the great branches of it."

Again he would tell them: "The Kingdom is like yeast. A housewife took some and mixed it into three cupfuls of flour. By and by it was all risen."

Among those who stood to listen to Jesus were two sets of brothers. The sons of Jonas had come to Capernaum from Bethsaida: Andrew was a well-built swarthy man, expert in fishing. When he first heard Jesus, he felt strangely drawn to him and he rushed off to fetch his brother Simon. "Come, Simon, and hear this new preacher. We saw him one day at the Jordan where John baptized, and he also was baptized in the river. Never have I heard any man speak as he does. You must come and hear him." Simon was a year or two older than Andrew and, like him, a fisherman. Their faces were tanned with the wind and the sun; they had all the simplicity of men who had spent many long nights on the water waiting patiently for the fish. They were lean and strong, and both of them godly men. They had both joined the movement of John the Baptist and looked forward eagerly to the arrival of that mysterious One of whom John had spoken. Simon was normally an impetuous man and he might have been expected to hurry with Andrew to listen to Jesus of Nazareth. But John's imprisonment had laid a heavy load upon Simon's heart; he wondered whether after all anything new would emerge from the prophetic work of John. He wasn't sure what a carpenter from Nazareth could do. But Andrew was excited. He talked about the different tone he had detected in the message of Jesus. "I tell you, Simon, you must come. He talks about 'the gospel of God.' Never a word about the fire of judgment and the hot breath of the divine vengeance. He says that the Kingdom of God is here at the door and it is as if something

tremendous is about to happen. I wonder . . . I wonder
. . . " "All right," replied his brother, "to please you I'll
come and hear him." So Andrew and Simon stood and
heard the preaching of Jesus and spoke briefly with him.

The second pair of brothers were also fishermen. Their
father, Zebedee, had several boats, and employed men to
work for him. The boys were younger than Andrew, and
all four had become close friends. Indeed James was with
Andrew the very first time they heard Jesus. He too had
responded favorably to the preaching and brought his
brother, John, with him. It was impossible to miss the four
fishermen in the crowd that gathered to hear him, and soon
Jesus knew them pretty well. James and John were high-
strung youths, "the sons of thunder," as some of their friends
said. But each was religious, each looked for the day when
God would indeed rule in the land. It was their ambition
to find a place in any movement that promoted that day, so
they had quickly joined John the Baptist. In their home
their mother had encouraged them to be devoted men of
God, and they had found an example of diligence and
humility in their father's life and character. One other fisherman whom they persuaded to join them was Philip of
Bethsaida, and he too became a listener.

It was certainly true that Jesus spoke quite differently
from John. The one had shouted and implored, the other
was quiet and his words had charm. John had harped on a
single theme and he seldom strayed far from it; Jesus
sounded like a poet and he had many themes. John reminded people of Elijah, Jesus reminded them of the poet
Isaiah, who had written:

> "How beautiful upon the mountains
>   are the feet of the herald
> Who brings good news of peace,
>   news of salvation,

> Who says to Zion,
>   'Your God has become King.' . . .
> Break into singing together,
>   you waste places of Jerusalem!
> For the Lord has comforted his people,
>   he has redeemed Jerusalem."

Of course there was always the cynic who listened politely, then muttered: "It's all poetry. He is just another preacher of pious platitudes. They have recited these things in Israel for a hundred years and nothing has happened, except that preachers like John get thrown into jail." And the agents of Herod and Pilate said: "Let him talk. All this about 'God at the door' is just preacher's jargon. Where is the proof of it? Where is the fire and lightning of judgment? Where is the royal power and glory? Caesar and Herod have nothing to fear from this obscure carpenter out of Nazareth!"

Jesus continued to tell his stories to those who came.

"You remember what is said in Scripture: 'As the earth puts forth her shoots, and as a garden makes the seed that is sown in it to spring up, so the Lord God shall make righteousness and praise to spring up before all the nations.' My friends, this is what God is doing now. He has been busy for many years before this and now he is bringing the harvest. God reigns, and nothing can prevent the growth of his Kingdom. It is as if a man sowed seed in his land, then slept by night and rose with the day. The seed sprouted and grew, he knew not how. By its own action the land brought the harvest: first a blade, then an ear, then the full grain in the ear. When the fruit allows, he puts in the sickle at once, for the harvest has arrived. I tell you, the time has now arrived. He that has ears to hear, let him hear!"

Andrew and his friends were still unable to see where Jesus fitted into the picture. There was no sign of that

mighty successor whom John had foretold. Jesus clearly did
not fill the bill, for he was persuasive and loving in all his
ways. He never blustered and he did not threaten. Information that men brought from Nazareth spoke only of a
humble, pious son whom everyone respected, though it was
admitted that Jesus had no peer in his knowledge of the
Bible and his religious convictions. Already Capernaum had
detected a note in his message that was missing in the con-
ventional preaching of the rabbis. Jesus was quite sure of
God and unambiguous in his declaration about the Kingdom. But he was also unusual, for his words had a teasing
quality that made one ponder their deeper meaning; and
Jesus seemed always to lay on his hearers the responsibility
of deciding what they would do with the word.

One day Simon turned to the others and said: "I'm going
off to fish. Nothing is happening and it looks as if nothing
is going to happen. But at least a man can fish and earn a
living. Perhaps we'll be lucky and have a fine catch to sell
at the wharf. Even if that miserly customs collector Levi
squeezes out of us more duty than he is entitled to, we can
always manage when there are more fish in the lake."

That night the sons of Jonas and the sons of Zebedee
went fishing. They fished all night, but they caught nothing.

Next morning, disappointed and touchy, they were busy
cleaning and repairing their nets, boats drawn close to the
shore, when Jesus of Nazareth appeared. After he had been
talking for a while, the crowds that pressed on him
threatened to push him into the water. Jesus saw the fishermen at work and made his way to them. "Simon," he said,
"would you mind if I borrowed your boat for a while? If you
would row me out a bit, I could preach to this multitude
from the boat. Otherwise I'm going to get pretty wet!"
"Certainly, sir," said Simon, and he rowed Jesus out some
way from the land.

That day Jesus told his listeners how happy were those who turned to God in the new age that had come.

"Happy are you poor, for yours is the Kingdom.

Happy are you who truly hunger, for you will be satisfied.

Happy are you who weep today, for then you will rejoice."

Then he went on to teach them the right way to fulfill the laws of God:

"When you give donations to charities,

Don't trumpet it abroad in the streets and synagogues; that is what hypocrites do.

They want to be praised by men, not by God.

Well, that is precisely what they get!

When *you* give donations to charities,

Hide from your left hand what your right is doing.

Keep them secret from men,

And God will reward you."

From the crowd someone called out: "We are unlettered men, but we want to do our duty to God. Tell us how we should pray." "Yes, I will tell you," answered Jesus.

"When you pray,

Don't mumble a lot of words, standing publicly at street corners and in the synagogues; that is what hypocrites do.

They want to be seen of men and to be praised by men.

Amen, I tell you; that is all they get!

When *you* pray,

Go into your own room and shut the door.

Pray privately to God,

and God will reward you."

When the teaching was over for the day, Jesus turned to Simon, thanking him for the boat. "Launch out now," he added, "and let down your nets in the deeper water of the lake for a catch." Simon looked at this teacher who thought he could tell experienced fishermen their business. "I don't think so," he said. "You see, sir, Andrew and I, with our partners, James and John, were out all last night fishing, and we caught nothing." "Nevertheless," said Jesus, "launch out, for this day you are going to catch fish." Simon shrugged his shoulders and had half a mind to say something derogatory about carpenters who should stick to their benches; but he caught a look in the face of Jesus and knew at once that he must do what this strange man told him. He gave the word and Andrew rowed out the boat. Where Jesus indicated, Simon let down the nets and at once he had a catch. "Help, help," he cried to the others, "all the fish in the lake seem to be here." When it looked as if the nets would burst and alone they could not cope with the weight of fish, they called over the water to the sons of Zebedee: "James! Ho, there, James and John! Hurry across and help us." Yet scarcely with the help of the others and of Jesus could they haul the nets to the shore. They were amazed and shaken beyond reason. "It's a miracle," they gasped. And Simon fell down at the feet of Jesus crying, "Sir, sir, depart from me, for I am a sinful man." But Jesus gently laid his hand on Simon and drew him to his feet. Looking at the four men, he said to them: "Lads, I need you for a greater work than this. Come you with me, Andrew and Simon; come you with me, James and John. Come with me as I tell the people of Galilee the great good news of the Kingdom of God. For it is here at their door. God is breaking in upon the lives of men and nothing can ever be the same again. Come with me, whom God has called to preach this Kingdom, and I will make you fishers of men for God's sake."

And from that hour these four went with Jesus and were his men. His hand upon them was like the very hand of God.

The Wonder of All Galilee

5 THIS SABBATH DAY there seemed to be an unusual crowd of men and women going down the streets of Capernaum to the synagogue. Dignified fathers tried to keep their families in order, but there wasn't much use in trying: the boys and girls ran about excitedly and the dark eyes of the women under their veils were bright and eager. People from Bethsaida, who had rowed across on Friday afternoon before sundown and stayed with friends, were also to be seen in the crowd. Here and there a Roman uniform stood out, for there were soldiers who rather enjoyed the simple prayers and happy singing of Jewish worship and came from time to time to share in it. The special interest of this day was that the ruler of the synagogue had invited Jesus to preach after the reading of the Law and the Prophets. Everyone wanted to hear his message of the Kingdom, for one never knew what events might be in the making.

Jesus loved the house of prayer and went regularly to Sabbath worship wherever he was. Today he was very glad to have this opportunity to preach, and very simply he tried to teach his listeners that their fathers' God was at this very moment working in Israel to fulfill the dreams of ages, to establish his Kingdom, to bring them the joys and blessings of abundant life. This was refreshing and exciting teaching! The congregation felt at once that they had never heard anyone quite like this. For Jesus spoke with assurance as well as simplicity. He did not, like most preachers, string off a long list of teachers on whose authority he had to rely. He taught them directly from his heart and gave people the impression that he lived very close to God.

"I am bringing you good news," said Jesus. "I want you to open your eyes to see God at work and to open your ears to hear his word. Our first duty is to love him with all our heart, with all our soul, and with all our strength. Our next duty is to leave no one unloved—no one. We should care for each because the Lord our God cares for all. This is wise and proper, and by acting in this way we shall bring peace to our land and happiness to many who are downcast. As the shepherd goes looking for the lost sheep and rejoices when he finds it, so does God care for his children.

"You may have heard the saying, 'You are to love your neighbor but hate your enemy.' But I tell you to love your enemies and pray for those who persecute you. So will you be the sons of God in heaven, who sends his rain on the just and the unjust. Or does the sun shine only on the good and not on the evil? If you love those who love you, what's the virtue in that? Even scoundrels do as much! If you are friendly only to your friends, what's special about that? Even the ungodly do as much! I tell you, if you would inherit the Kingdom, you must do more than that. You must be perfect, as God in heaven is perfect."

Now in the synagogue that day there was a man who was mentally deranged. The general opinion was that he was under the control of a "demon," because quite unexpectedly he would be thrown to the ground in a fit, foaming and cursing. Something in the words or appearance of Jesus disturbed him during the service and suddenly he cried out: "What have you to do with us, Jesus of Nazareth? I recognize you, I know you to be the Holy One from God. You've come to destroy us." Jesus came down to the man and with a word rebuked him. "Be quiet," he said. "Be quiet, you unclean spirit; come out of him and let the man be," he commanded. And there was at once a shrieking that seemed to split the roof; the man fell down in a convulsion. Jesus stooped over him and lifted him gently to his feet. When the man got up, he was perfectly sane and quiet.

"What on earth is this?" people said. From the gallery the women craned their necks to see better what was going on. Officials hurried the man out and told him to go straight home. Jesus smiled and left with his friends Simon and Andrew, James and John. But the men gazed wonderingly at Jesus and whispers could be heard: "Who is this man? And what kind of new teaching is this we have listened to this day? For Jesus of Nazareth both speaks and acts with an authority the like of which we have not seen before in Capernaum!"

Jesus had no home of his own in the town and he had gratefully accepted an invitation from Simon and his wife to stay with them. When they arrived at the house they found that Simon's mother-in-law was ill with fever. Still astonished themselves at what they had seen in the synagogue, they told Jesus about the sickness. Jesus went over to the sick woman, spoke to her, and raised her by the hand. She was quite well again and helped to serve the meal.

Later that same afternoon, as soon as the Sabbath Day had ended at sunset and it was once more lawful for religious Jews who observed the Commandments to travel on business, great crowds gathered in the courtyard of Simon's flat-roofed house. They brought the sick and many who were in mental distress to be touched by this new healer. And he healed them all, with prayer to God and thanksgiving. Evil spirits fled at the sound of his holy voice. Tired and self-centered men and women found refreshment in one who seemed to take upon himself their burdens, their anxieties, and even their sins. He brought God and the love of God very close to them, and in this love they began to get well physically and spiritually. Hope brought strength; serenity in mind calmed their fevers and their fears. "Did I not tell you," Jesus would say, with some wonder in his voice, "did I not tell you that God had begun his marvelous work and that his Kingdom was at your doors? Will you see? Will you hear?"

Early the next morning Simon's wife roused him in some distress. "The Master isn't here," she said. "His bed hasn't been slept in, either. What can have happened to him? Where has he gone?" Simon tried to reassure her as well as he could, but he himself was pretty anxious. Already there were signs that more people were being brought to Jesus for healing. They must find the Master at once. "Andrew, Andrew," he called. "Wake up, man, and help me. Jesus

has gone, and we don't know where he is." So in an outburst
of concern Simon and Andrew, with some other friends, ran
up the street looking for Jesus. At last they spied him
coming down a hill path and rushed forward to surround
him with their anxiety. "Master, Master," shouted Simon.
"O how relieved we are to find you! Where have you been?
Are you coming home now? The whole world is looking for
you. Everyone wants you to do something for him. Come
with us, come quickly. O it is so good to see you again! Are
you all right? Come on!" Jesus very quietly but very firmly
said no. "I have been in the hills all night, Simon. I have
been with my Father and I have work to do for him elsewhere. We must move on and tell the great good news of the
Kingdom in the neighboring villages. You shall come with
me, Andrew and Simon. Find James, John, and Philip and
we will set off this very day. For it was for this purpose that I
came forth on my mission."

The men collected what they needed for their journey,
said good-by to families and friends, and departed. On the
way they heard a cry: "Unclean! Unclean!" and saw a man
emerge from scrub by the roadside. The disciples kept their
distance, for this was a poor creature branded with the
loathsome disease of leprosy, who was forbidden to come
near healthy people. But Jesus approached him, and the
leper said, "Sir, if you will, you can cleanse me." And then,
to the horror of his disciples, the Master touched the kneel-
ing man and said: "I will; be clean. Go and do what the law
requires; and see that you tell no man who it was that
touched you." With loud protestations of joy the healed
leper ran off, and the disciples followed with a strange
wonder in their eyes. To Chorazin and Nain, to Cana and
Sepphoris, they went, and Jesus preached: "I bring you
good news, the good news of God's Kingdom which is at
your doors!"

Wherever he went people were astonished by the wisdom and charm of his words; they were so simple and yet so profound. He was poet and prophet in one. His stories were vivid and pointed. And what spiritual power he brought to unhappy and disappointed men and women! What fun he had with the children! O there had never been such a prophet as this, their own Galilean out of Nazareth, and they were proud of him. Jesus himself rejoiced at the response he received. He made friends everywhere and attracted other followers who wanted to join the brothers of Capernaum and Philip of Bethsaida; among the new men was another Simon, a man who had been identified with those patriots called Zealots who preached armed rebellion against the Romans and the setting up of a Jewish state. There were women too who found that Jesus was considerate and willing to help them; he showed none of that feeling of male superiority common among the Jews. Joanna, the wife of Chuza, a steward of King Herod Antipas, was one of the women who learned to love Jesus for his goodness and his help.

One day Jesus said to his disciples, "I am going home to Nazareth, for it is fitting that I should preach there too."

Word of his coming preceded him, and the town seemed to be ready to give him an uproarious welcome. He was a distinguished preacher now; stories had poured in about the wonderful cures he had wrought; and now here he was in person! Was he still the village carpenter they had known so well and respected? What message would he have for Nazareth?

Jesus' first care was to see his mother and the rest of the family, and it was a great joy to them all that he had returned. Then on the Sabbath they all went, as their custom was, to the synagogue. Jesus had been invited to preach. After the psalms of praise, the prayers, and the readings from the sacred rolls, Jesus rose from his place and went to sit in the seat of the rabbi, and from it he taught them his gospel of the Kingdom.

He told them how God had called him to take up the work of preaching the good news after the ministry of John the Baptist had been arrested. He recalled to their attention the wonderful prophecies that told how God would care for his chosen people, healing their diseases, bearing their sorrows, pardoning their offenses. "All this is happening now through my work," he said. And he went on to relate some of his famous parables about the seed and the fruit, about the yeast, about the mustard seed.

Nazareth reacted very strangely to his appearance and his words. Some could not get over the charm with which he preached: "Why, he is just our village carpenter!" they said. Some wondered at the wisdom and spiritual depth of his teaching, but instead of thanking God for it and accepting it humbly, they wanted to know, "Where did he get all this learning?" Others were frankly cynical and unbelieving: "Who does he think he is? Isn't this Mary's son, whose brothers and sisters live in our village? Is he any better than the rest of us?"

And so controversy arose. What was worse, even the members of his own family did not take him seriously and it was suggested in the family circle that all the excitement had "gone to his head." Nobody wanted to be healed that evening. They didn't believe in Jesus and so there was nothing he could do for them. The lines of communication had broken down; his hands could not reach them, for they drew back from him; his words could not reach them, for they stopped their ears against him. When he said to some: "It is the old story. A prophet receives honor except in his native place," tempers began to flare. There were angry words and they accused him of conceit and misrepresentation. As the darkness came on, the mob got out of hand and tried to seize Jesus, thinking to throw him over a precipice outside the village. But Jesus, calm and prayerful, stood upright among them and his eyes flashed with the power of the divine Spirit, daring a single man there to lay hands on him whom God had called! And they flinched from him, not able to bear that matchless purity. They saw in his face the rebuke of holy love, and they fell back. Jesus walked unharmed through the ungrateful and antagonistic mob, shepherded his disciples, and left the town, in deep sorrow and distress. His own folk had rejected him! His home had turned him out and rejected his gospel of the Kingdom! That night Jesus spent in lonely vigil, praying to the Father.

Soon the little company returned to Simon's house in Capernaum, where they had a warm welcome. The customs officer at the wharf in Capernaum was a young man called Levi, the son of Alphaeus. The primary business of anybody in this profession was not gathering the tolls for Herod Antipas so much as feathering his own nest. Whenever it suited his pocket he would accept bribes and look the other way. This was very offensive to decent Jews, for they valued honesty and trustworthiness. But Levi was disliked also because he was forever mixing with the foreigners, the Gentile strangers who worshiped other gods and laughed at the strict rules under which Jews had to live. "I might as well be hanged for a sheep as for a lamb," laughed Levi. "They hate me anyway because I have a job with the government of Herod and they don't like my easy attitude to money. What do I care? I'm as good as they are and I have a far better time than most of them. If only they would admit it, many of them really envy me, for everyone wants fun and pleasure." So Levi went his own way and his friends were men and women who paid little attention to the moral demands of the Jewish law.

One advantage Jesus had over the critics of young Levi: he loved people so much that he could understand them. He could see much farther down into the real person. And Jesus had seen more in Levi than met the ordinary eye. He saw a man with a zest for life; a friendly man; a youth who believed, and believed wrongly, that religion always put a damper on love and laughter and good fellowship. The face that Levi wore was not the truest indication of his nature: for he had instinctively put on the hard, suspicious face of the official who knew that a great many people, even respectable citizens, would try to get by him without paying toll or duty. Levi was in some respects what other men had made him, and they were not all bad men. Jesus knew all about Levi, and took the trouble to speak to him in a friendly fashion as occasion offered.

Then one day Jesus suddenly appeared at the customs booth, looked Levi straight in the eye, and said to him: "Levi, I need you. Come and follow me!"

Levi was utterly astonished. But to his own surprise he looked Jesus also in the eye and heard himself saying, "Yes, I'll come."

How the town talked about this new accession to the company of Jesus' disciples! "Fishermen and tax collectors!" said the self-righteous. "Strange bedfellows for a prophet of God! A friend of the friends of Gentiles: what is he up to?" Even the people who looked on Jesus with particular favor were taken aback by the manner in which he insisted on following his practice of leaving nobody unloved. It was so unconventional, so drastic, so idealistic!

Neither Jesus nor Levi cared much who was offended. Levi was quite delighted to find that Jesus wanted his help, and he looked forward to the new adventure. For he had still no idea to what this would lead. He was so pleased indeed that he prepared a dinner, to which he invited many of his old friends and several intimates of Jesus. And everyone enjoyed it; the food was excellent and the company brotherly. Jesus himself entered into the spirit of the evening wholeheartedly.

But this was too much for the "good people" of the town. They mocked this gathering of "birds of a feather"; they condemned the new teacher for associating with the riffraff. Jesus could not endure this without reply. To his critics he said: "You used to complain about John the Baptist because he fasted too much, and some of you said that he must be under a demon's control. Now you say that I am a glutton and a drunkard, a friend to tax collectors and sinners. Listen! those who are in good health don't need a doctor; those who are sick do. I did not come to call the righteous, but to call sinners."

So the self-righteous withdrew, uncomfortable but unconvinced, for this was the strangest kind of piety and the queerest method of preparing people for the wonderful Kingdom of God of which they had ever heard. But Levi and others like him were pleased and sorry at the same time: glad that they had found a new kind of God in this prophet from Nazareth; sorry that they had waited so long to discover how good life could be when it was lived according to the love about which their new Master preached so much. They knew very well that they had been sick souls and that Jesus had brought them healing. They knew that they had been prodigals, and they would recall Jesus' story:

"A certain man had two sons, and the younger boy said to his father, 'Father, divide to me now the share of the estate that will fall to me.' So he divided his property between the two sons. Shortly afterward the younger son sold his possessions and set off with his money for a far country. There he squandered it in vicious living. After he had lost all his money there came a famine in that country and he began to be in want. So he attached himself to a citizen of the land who kept swine and became a pigherd. Sometimes he was so famished that he would gladly have eaten of the pigs' swill, but no one gave him anything.

"At last he came to himself and said: 'Why, my father has many paid servants who get food enough and to spare; yet here am I perishing from hunger! I will arise and go to my father, and I will say to him: "Father, I have sinned before God and before you. I am no longer worthy to be called your son. Make me like one of the paid servants and I shall be content." '

"So he arose and came to his father. But while he was still far off, his father saw him on the road, had compassion on him, and ran and took him in his arms and kissed him. Then the boy said: 'Father, I have sinned before God and before you. I no longer deserve to be called your son.' But his father called to the servants: 'Quick! bring the best tunic and put it on him; put a ring on his hand and sandals on his feet. Kill the fatted calf and let us eat and be merry. For this my son was dead and is alive again; he was lost and is found.' And they made merry.

"Now the elder son was in the field, and as he came home he heard music and dancing in the house. 'What does this mean?' he asked one of the servants. 'Your brother is home, sir, and your father has killed the fatted calf because he has received him back safe and sound.' Then he was angry and would not join the party. His father came out and begged him to join them, but he replied churlishly: 'Look, for many years I have served you; never was I disobedient to your wishes, yet you have never given me so much as a young goat that I might make merry with my friends. But as soon as this your "son" comes back, you kill the fat calf for him!' 'My son,' answered the father, 'you are always with me, and everything that I have is yours. Yet it was right to make merry and be glad, for this your "brother" was dead and is alive again; he was lost and is found.' "

Once, after a visit to the Decapolis country across the lake, Jesus and his disciples landed in the neighborhood of Capernaum. Immediately a synagogue officer called Jairus rushed up to Jesus. He was in obvious distress and cried: "My little girl is dying! Please come and lay your hands on her so that she may get well." Jesus consented and a crowd followed them. Among them was a woman who had suffered for many years from frequent discharges of blood. If only I could touch the tassel of his robe, he could heal me too! she thought. In the press of people around Jesus it was easy to do this and she was about to slip away, timid and fearful of making a scene. But Jesus knew at once that someone had touched him purposely and he felt that power had flowed out from him. He stopped. "Who touched me?" Simon and the others suggested that all kinds of people might have touched him, but Jesus insisted that someone had done more than rub casually against him. The woman realized now that she could not escape him and threw herself down at his feet, tearfully admitting what she had done. Jesus was very gracious to her. "Daughter," he said, "your trust in me has healed you. Go and be at peace."

Just then a messenger from the home of Jairus caught up with them. "It's too late," he reported. "The little girl is dead; you needn't trouble the rabbi any further." But Jesus paid no heed to the message; it was never too late for his work. "You are not to be afraid," he said to Jairus; "have faith in me." When they got to the house, the professional mourning women were already there, making the loud lamentations demanded by custom. It was quite pitiful to see the face of the stricken father and the grief of his wife. Jesus took the parents, and three close friends, Simon, James, and John, and as he brushed past the wailing women, he told them to be quiet. "The child is not dead but sleeping." They were naturally astonished, but they went on doing what they had been hired to do.

Inside the girl's room Jesus crossed over to the bed and prayed beside it; then he took the child by the hand, saying, "Little girl, I tell you to arise!" She awoke and sat up in bed. "Give her something to eat," said Jesus to the overjoyed parents, and quickly he went away with the disciples.

Now there were very many men and women throughout Galilee who needed Jesus and the new life he could bring. This was how his Father's Kingdom was coming into its own in the land. Not by might, but by the spirit of love, sinful people were discovering what God's service really meant. But Jesus could not be in every place at once and to take the gospel into all Galilee, into Samaria and Judea, he must have assistants to preach and act in God's name.

Jesus therefore chose twelve men from among his intimate disciples: the brothers from Capernaum; Levi; Philip of Bethsaida; Simon the Zealot; Thomas the Twin; Judas Iscariot; Bartholomew; Thaddaeus; and James, the son of Alphaeus. There was one for each of the twelve tribes of Israel, and they would be living symbols to the nation of what God was doing. Through the ministry of Jesus he was liberating them from bondage to self-interest; he was enabling them to lose their lives and to find life in loving service for others; he was making them fit to declare the glory of the Lord before all nations. Jesus knew now that the road would be difficult, since even Nazareth had been cold and hostile and the leaders of religion in Capernaum had been disappointed by the kind of company the new prophet kept.

To the Twelve therefore he gave these commissions:

"Go out two by two and preach the good news of the Kingdom as you have heard me preach. Call your listeners

...in to God that he may use them to glorify him.
...from me spiritual authority over unclean spirits
...u have seen me do, bring joy and healing to the
...he distressed. Take nothing else: neither food nor
money. Make one tunic do; wear sandals and carry a staff.
You are to be the salt of the land and its light; so shine
before men that they will glorify my Father in heaven. In
any place where you are welcomed, stay as long as is necessary and convenient. Where you are rejected, shake off the
very dust for a witness against it. Amen, I tell you, it will
be more tolerable in the day of judgment for ancient Sodom
or Gomorrah, cities of wickedness, than for such a place.
For he that receives you is receiving me; and he that receives me is receiving not me alone, but also him that sent
me."

So they went out with God, and in the power of God they
preached and healed as their Master had commanded them.
When they returned, bringing exciting reports, Jesus rejoiced and cried out in ecstasy: "I saw the prince of evil fall
from the skies like a lightning flash! Nevertheless, come
apart with me into a quiet place where we may be refreshed;
for alas! many set store more on the healing of the body
than the cure of sick hearts, and many are offended by us."

One day Jesus was back again in Capernaum, and news of
his arrival spread quickly. Soon a large crowd had gathered
in the yard of the house where he was staying. Along came
four men carrying a pallet on which lay a man who was
paralyzed. They tried every way, but could not get near
Jesus. Nothing daunted, the four men with their burden
climbed onto the roof and proceeded to dig a hole in it.
Then, to the astonishment of all in the room, they lowered
the bed right to the feet of Jesus. Jesus looked up with a
smile at the faces peering through the hole in the roof, then
he looked long and searchingly into the face of the paralytic.

At length he spoke very tenderly to the sufferer. "Son," he said, "your sins are forgiven!"

What a change this caused in the atmosphere! The faces up above were puckered in dismay: this was not what they had interrupted the sermon for! The whole company wondered what Jesus meant, and in one corner some learned scribes, teachers of the law, were so horrified at such language that they frowned and their eyes said to one another, "Why, this is blasphemy!" Jesus read their thoughts. "You are put out," he called over to them; "you do not believe that the Son of Man has authority on earth to forgive sins. But I know it and I possess that right. Will it become more credible to you if I tell this man to take up his bed and go home?" With these words he turned to the man and said, "Rise, take up your bed and go home." And the man did so! "Glory be to God!" said the people. "We never saw the like of this." But the scribes were angry and afraid, for the words of Jesus seemed to them more daring than any mortal man had the right to use.

About this time two disciples came from a visit to their master, John the Baptist, who was still in prison, and said to Jesus, "Are you the One who is to come?" "See for yourselves," was the answer. "See how the prophecies are being fulfilled: there are blind who see and deaf who hear; there are lame who walk and unclean who are cleansed; dead souls are coming to life again, and to the poor the gospel is being preached." The men went away, wondering.

Jesus continued to instruct his own disciples. "The Kingdom," he told them, "is like treasure hidden in a field. A man found this treasure and hid it again; then he took himself off, sold all that he had, and bought that field. It is like a merchant who traded in fine pearls. Once he found a pearl of superlative value. So he went off, sold all that he had, and bought that pearl." And, because opposition was growing, he said: "To you it has been granted to receive the secret of the Kingdom. But to others it is like a riddle; for they can see but do not perceive the meaning; they can hear, but they do not understand. If they did, they would turn to my Father and be pardoned."

Shortly after this the hand of Herod struck once more. At a regal feast in his palace, Salome, the daughter of Herodias, danced for his entertainment. All the nobility were there and Herod lorded over them in Oriental magnificence. "Girl, you excel in beauty every woman but your mother and you dance divinely. Come now, I would reward you for the pleasure you have given us. Up to the half of my kingdom will I give you. What will you have?" "What shall I ask for, Mother?" said Salome; and Herodias replied, "Ask for the head of John the Baptist on a platter." When the king heard this, he was greatly troubled at heart, for he was superstitious and wasn't at all sure that it would be wise to get rid of a prophet at this time and in this way. Yet, for the sake of his honor and the rash promise made before these arrogant aristocrats, he dared not refuse. John was put to death in his prison; they cut off his head and brought it on a platter to Salome, the dancing princess.

The news brought a shudder of dread to many in Galilee. What was the use of prophets and their talk of the Kingdom of God if this was what happened?

Jesus too was distressed, and he resolved to withdraw into a lonely place to seek the counsel of his Father. If John had to suffer like this, what about the Son who was to be to Israel a Messiah?

Who Is He?

6 THOMAS the Twin and Simon the Zealot were walking together as they followed Jesus. "Friend Thomas," said Simon, "I am puzzled to know what our Master is up to. In some ways he is a very strange leader. But I came with him because he persuaded me that God's Kingdom was really forcing its way into the life of Israel. These last months I have seen such signs and wonders—and so have you—that I

am still convinced he is our God-sent leader. Who else could be the Messiah? And yet he does nothing to gain power in the nation; he recruits no army; and he lets foxy Herod get away with the murder of John the Baptist."

"Simon, I was convinced too; but like you I have become doubtful. It is so hard to see how the campaign is going to work out. Does he have a plan? Is he really the Messiah whom we expected? I know that he has tremendous authority over men and over demons. Do you remember that Sabbath Day when the Pharisees complained because Jesus let us rub the grains of corn?" "I remember it well," said Simon. "He quoted King David to them. If David could raid the sacred house and eat the very loaves of the divine Presence, why shouldn't he and his men eat the corn? How regal he sounded! It was as if someone greater than David had come!"

"I grant you that. I recall what he said to those who criticized his healings on the Sabbath. 'The Son of Man is lord of the Sabbath, because the Sabbath was made for man.' But I don't understand why everything moves so slowly; and I am puzzled about his references to the Son of Man. So far as I know, the Son of Man is one who some say will come down on the clouds of heaven with bands of angels. What on earth does he mean? Who is he?"

"I don't know any more than you do, Simon. He tells us to seek first the Kingdom and everything else will be added to us. He commands us to serve God alone and not mammon or any other idol; and I can understand something of that. One has to be single-minded for a great enterprise. Haven't we left all to follow him? Perhaps we do not yet understand what God means to him. He is often out all night in prayer. His whole life is determined by this practice. Suppose we ask him to help us further with our prayers? Jesus is a very wonderful man and we must stick by him."

That evening by the campfire Jesus answered Thomas and Simon.

"Prayer is like a child coming to his parents to thank them for their care and ask them for help. God made us and he watches over us, just as he watches over the birds and the flowers and everything he has made. There isn't a sparrow that falls to the ground without his knowledge; there isn't a hair of your heads that hasn't been counted. Look at the anemones, here today and gone tomorrow; they do not toil and they do not spin; yet, I tell you, even Solomon in all his glory was not arrayed like one of them.

"Trust God, therefore. Ask, and you will receive; seek, and you will find; knock, and the door will be opened to you. Do you think an earthly father would give his boy a serpent when he asked for a fish, or a scorpion when he asked for an egg? How much more will the Heavenly Father give good things to them that ask him!"

"Master," said Andrew, "John the Baptist used to teach his disciples a prayer. Would you give us a prayer that we might use?"

"Certainly, Andrew. This is how you should pray:
"Father,
    May thy name be sanctified:
    May thy kingdom come:
    May thy will be done:
    as in heaven, so in earth.
    Give us this day bread enough for a day.
    And forgive us our trespasses,
    as we forgive our debtors.
    Lead us not into the tribulation, but deliver us
        from the power of the evil one.

"You must remember," he continued, "that God cannot forgive you if you refuse to forgive one another. Happy are the merciful, for they shall receive mercy. Let me tell you a story about prayer:

"Most unexpectedly friends came to visit a family late at night. You can imagine the consternation of the housewife when she found that her cupboard was bare. She fussed and she fretted and insisted that her husband must run up the street to beg from her neighbor. It was midnight, but he had to go! With a great to-do he awakened his neighbor and asked him for some bread. 'For,' he explained, 'unexpected guests have arrived at our house and we have nothing to set before them.' His neighbor was sleepy and annoyed. 'Go away,' he called, 'it's your own fault or your wife's fault. What do you mean, disturbing decent folk at this time of night?' But the man would not budge. He was determined that he would get something to take home. At last, if only to get rid of such persistence, his neighbor rose and gave him what he wanted.

"You must never give up when you pray. And remember that you cannot serve two masters; for either you will love the one and hate the other, or you will adhere to one and despise the other. God must come first; we are to love God with all our heart and with all our soul and with all our strength."

Meantime the people had discovered that Jesus and his disciples had withdrawn and they went looking for them. For most of them still placed great hope in Jesus, despite the cruel death of John and the power of Herod. So many tales had been told of what wonderful things Jesus had said and done that there were some who openly asked if Jesus must not be their Messiah. "Surely he is our king," they said. Then they must expect him to proclaim himself soon and to gather his forces to drive out the alien rulers of Rome and Edom. "Death to the Romans! death to the Herodians!" some began to shout. And some among them who had but recently returned from celebrating the Passover feast at Jerusalem, the feast that recalled God's deliverance of

Israel from Egyptian slavery, stirred up the eager crowd as they followed after Jesus. "Blessed be the kingdom that is to come, the kingdom of our father David! Hosanna in the heavens!"

Before very long they caught up with the disciples and surged round Jesus to hear what he would say to them.

"You have come out to see me here; a few short months ago it was to see and hear the Baptist. What did you really go out to see in the desert places of Judea and the fords of Jordan? A blade of grass blown by the wind? A man clothed in the garments of luxury? Gorgeous dresses and luxury living are to be found in king's palaces! What really did you go out to see? A prophet? Yes, but I tell you, he was more than a prophet! I tell you, no man has yet arisen greater than John the Baptist. For he was the messenger sent beforehand by the Lord our God. And now the Kingdom of God is in the midst, though many see it not. They ask for signs and do not recognize what is being done right before their very eyes. They ask for authorities, and cannot appreciate what is being said to them. But perhaps with you it will be different."

Far on into the evening Jesus taught them that fine spring day, filled with compassion for them. They were such a mixed group of men, with all kinds of wrong ideas and ideals in their heads. They seemed to him like sheep that had no shepherd or an army that had no commander. They were obviously curious and excited; they were ready to follow the kind of leader they wanted and they thought of the divine Kingdom not as the rule of love but as the rule of superhuman force. Nevertheless they had come, so he spent himself ministering to their needs of body and spirit.

Then Andrew and Philip came to him. "Master, it is late and the people are hungry and tired. Send them away to find food in the villages and farms round about." "Give them food yourselves," replied Jesus. At this they were amazed and protested: "Where on earth are we going to get the money to buy food for so many? The thing's impossible." "How many loaves do you have?" They went to find out and Andrew came back with the tally: "Five barley loaves and a couple of fish."

Jesus next commanded the disciples to arrange the crowd in orderly groups on the green grass. When this had been done, he made all keep silence while he offered prayer. He gave thanks to the Heavenly Father, the giver of all good gifts, for daily food and daily providence. He asked that everyone there might know the goodness of God and the nearness of his Kingdom; that this happy feast at the end of the day might prove to be a foretaste of the blessed feast they would share with all God's people when the Kingdom had won its full triumph.

Then he took the bread, broke it, and divided it to those nearest him; and he did the same with the fish. From hand to hand they passed the gifts he had blessed, and, to the astonishment of them all, there seemed to be no end to the supply. For everyone ate and was satisfied, and there was some left over, which the disciples gathered up that there might be no waste.

To the mystified multitude who had been taught and fed this seemed to be the marvelous sign they had waited for. Like Israel in the desert long ago, they had been fed with heavenly manna by the man of God. Soon voices began to express what they felt. "Hail, King-Messiah!" . . . "Is not this the Son of David?" . . . "Glory be to God who has sent us a king to lead us!" Voice after voice took up the joyful shouts and they began to sing their hosannas. Some wanted to seize Jesus there and then and acclaim him king. But Jesus would have none of it. He halted the multitude and peremptorily sent them home. None could face him. They turned on their heels and departed, their joy transformed into disillusionment.

Jesus withdrew his disciples and gave them orders to leave secretly at once for the other side of the lake. "There I shall meet you. Now I must go into the hills to pray."

That night a fierce storm developed and the disciples in their boat were nervous without their Master. The winds were so strong that they were driven far off their course and drawn close in to the shore near Bethsaida. Here in the mists before the dawn Jesus found them. As he walked toward them, the bewildered, exhausted men at first could not make out who or what it was; they thought it was a ghost or a mirage. But he called to them, "It is I, lads; don't be afraid," so they took him into the boat and with the sunrise made straight for their desired haven at Bethsaida.

As his ministry continued, Jesus used to think much of a parable that he told to his disciples in order to explain his patient perseverance in teaching. "A farmer," he had said, "went out to sow his field. Some of the seed fell by the wayside and the birds came and ate it up. Some of the seed fell on rocky ground, where there was little soil; for this reason it sprouted at once. But, when the sun rose in its strength, the seed was burned up; having no root, it simply withered. Other seed fell among thorns; the thorns grew up and suffocated it, so that it produced no fruit. But the rest of the seed fell on good ground, sprouted, and increased till the harvest. The yield from it was thirtyfold or sixtyfold or a hundredfold. He that has ears to hear, let him hear!"

He that has ears! There were so many who listened to his stories without any comprehension. They were concerned most of the time with this world and this world's goods, and had no care to have treasure in heaven. Satisfactions of the flesh were more to them than God and the love of God. So they altogether misunderstood what Jesus had to say about the Kingdom of God. They looked for armed rebellion; they wanted a Christ who was a sovereign like Caesar or Herod. Yet from the very beginning of his public work Jesus had never intended any such program. The people were deaf and blind. He knew also that the best of the religious leaders, the scrupulous party known as Pharisees, masters in the Scriptures and learned in the prophecies, had not rallied to his standard. They had been deeply offended by his claim to override the Sabbath law and to declare the forgiveness of sins. Jesus longed to teach the Pharisees the way of the Father's patient love; there was so much they had to give if only they could be freed from their self-righteous attitude and their spiritual snobbery. He was glad therefore to accept an invitation to supper from Simon, one of the Galilean Pharisees.

The meal was suddenly interrupted. Into the open courtyard where Simon and his guests were reclining burst a woman, her hair in disarray, her eyes red from weeping. She made straight for Jesus and flung herself sobbing at his feet, washing them, as it were, with her tears and then wiping them with her long, lovely hair.

The Pharisee of course was shocked by this display of emotion from a well-known prostitute. Did Jesus not recognize her? Did he not feel that, like Simon, he had been contaminated? The fact that Jesus made no attempt whatever to rebuke the woman was perhaps the most shocking thing of all in Simon's eyes. He muttered to himself, "If this Jesus were truly a prophet, he would know the sort of sinful woman she is; he wouldn't let her come near him!" Jesus remained perfectly still, and now the woman broke open a costly alabaster flask of very expensive perfume. The fragrant odor of it filled the whole yard. She kissed the feet of Jesus and anointed them with the perfume. Her only joy seemed to be thus to play the part of a loving servant.

Jesus had seen what was going through Simon's mind. "You have been offended, Simon, by the appearance of this woman, haven't you?" Simon's face was all scorn. "You have no compassion for her and you do not see that she is penitent. I know what she has been; I have seen her on the edge of the crowd, listening to the word. And because she has heard the word of God, calling her to repentance and love, she has come to me in gratitude.

"You, Simon, are my host. You are a Pharisee, but you do not trust me, you do not recognize my right to preach, and you do not accept my gospel. In your own eyes you are righteous, for you take all precautions not to transgress the laws and the traditions of your teachers. But what good do you do? What are you good for? I came to your home this evening, my friend, as your invited guest. Did you bother to do me the courtesies due to a guest? You did not. You provided no water that I might bathe my feet, but she has washed them with her tears and wiped them with her hair. Did you give me any welcome kiss? No, but since she came in she has been kissing my feet. You did not honor me with oil for my head, but she has anointed my feet with her perfume.

"And so I tell you this, Simon. She is indeed a great sinner, but her sins are forgiven. For she has learned to love God. She has heard the voice of God and responded!" Then he turned to the penitent woman and said graciously, "Go in peace; by your faith are you made whole." To the rest of the company he added: "Have I not told you that I am come to call sinners, not the righteous? He that is forgiven little will love little; she who has loved much has had a great forgiveness, and there is joy in heaven over one such penitent."

The party broke up, for the Pharisee and his friends could not agree with such doctrine. Who was this teacher that once again he should blaspheme by telling the woman that her sins were forgiven? No one could forgive sins except God. Who, then, was this Jesus?

The same question was being asked in the court of King Herod. His agents never took their eyes off Jesus in view of his early popularity. They knew that one of their customs officials had joined the group of disciples; and Chuza, one of the palace stewards, provided useful information which he obtained from his wife Joanna. When they asked at the court, "Who is the new preacher?" some said, "He is another Elijah!" Others said, "He seems to be like one of the ancient prophets." But the king in his superstition said, "I wonder if he can be John the Baptist risen from the dead?" "Redouble your precautions," was his order, "and see that there is no danger to the State or to our relations with the Romans."

The Pharisees began to dispute more and more with Jesus.

"Your disciples don't observe the ceremonial washings before meals," they complained. "Why don't your disciples fast as we do? . . . What sign will you give us that you have authority to preach and cast out demons?"

For his part Jesus grew ever more angry with their conceit and their conservative ways. "Hypocrites that you are," he answered them. "You are so concerned about the outside and so little about what is inside. Yet it is from within that evil thoughts come, and lust, theft, coveting, and all manner of deceit. It says in the law, 'You shall not commit adultery'; but I say to you, everyone who even looks at a woman with desire for her in his heart has already committed the sin of adultery. Moreover, you Pharisees virtually set your traditions above the law itself. Doesn't the Commandment say, 'Honor your father and your mother'? But by your interpretation a man has only to say that the money he should use for their support is corban, 'dedicated to God,' and he is freed from obeying the law. In this way you make the word of God void by the word of men! No sign will be given to this generation save the sign of the prophet Jonah. For he preached to Nineveh, and at his preaching Nineveh repented. The Son of Man has come preaching, but this generation has not repented."

"You are a madman," they countered bitterly. "You are the agent of Beelzebul, the prince of the demons!"

Jesus replied: "Something greater than Jonah is here, but you cannot see it. Something greater than the Temple is here, but you are blind. If a kingdom is divided against itself, it cannot stand. Why should Satan cast out Satan? No one enters a strong man's house to pillage his goods until first he overpowers the strong man; then he can plunder his house. Even so, by my works Satan is being overthrown and conquered! If I by the finger of God cast out demons, then the Kingdom of God is within your reach! But you fail to understand and you will have nothing to do with the love of God."

The finger of God! . . . authority to forgive sins! . . . stronger than Satan! . . . Lord over the Sabbath! . . . something greater than the very Temple of God! . . . who is this Son of Man he talks about? Who is this Jesus?

"He is getting dangerous," said the Herodians.

"He is a blasphemer," said the Pharisees.

And the two groups from that time forth took counsel together about the menace of Jesus and how they might be rid of him.

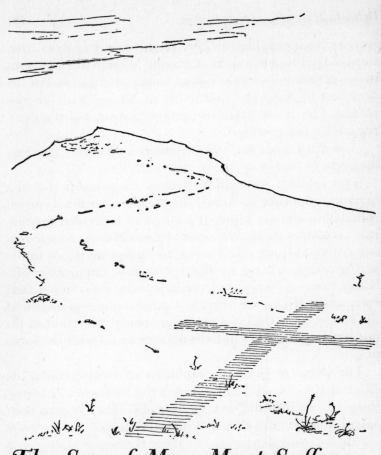

The Son of Man Must Suffer

7 JESUS KNEW perfectly well that his enemies were conspiring against him. It wasn't just that they couldn't understand the teaching he was offering. The Jews could not ignore what he was doing, for he had miraculous powers over sickness of body and mind; supernatural power within him lay ever ready to help men and women oppressed by forces of evil. They had to explain it. Well, some of the

Pharisees and some of the Herodians could explain it all right! "He must be in league with Satan." But for Jesus himself these were the mighty works of God, overruling in love and majesty, revealing to the wise and humble how it is that God reigns. God through Jesus was seeking graciously to show Israel a new kind of Kingdom, but they could not or would not understand. Jesus faced the issue squarely.

He knew that the Father was in very truth bringing in a new age, but the cost of it was bound to be far beyond all human comprehension. The Son had been accused of devilry! Men were conspiring against him. Now the synagogues of Galilee were being shut in his face, for the orthodox teachers would not allow him to "corrupt" their congregations. John the Baptist had been murdered by Herod, and Herod's partisans were joining with his other enemies to destroy Jesus too. Jesus knew it all, knew it better than his friends. For he could never compromise; the work must go on.

But what about his own disciples? Had they grasped the full import of his mission and method? Jesus knew that they had not. Simon the Zealot and Judas Iscariot were both planning for a kingdom of the Messiah exactly on the lines of other worldly kingdoms. They wanted a David or a Solomon. James and John, the sons of Zebedee, had heads filled with ideas of future glory; they were ambitious and wanted places of honor in his kingdom. Teaching and training them was slow and laborious work, but with these men he must persist; in these men he had faith.

Jesus resolved now to leave Galilee for a while. He journeyed northward toward the coast and visited Tyre and Sidon, two bustling ports. Then he led his followers into the territories of Philip the Tetrarch, brother of King Herod Antipas. Below Mt. Hermon, Philip had his capital at Caesarea Philippi, lovely city built by Herod the Great on the model of pagan cities. In the neighborhood of this place Jesus and the disciples encamped, and Jesus spent much time in prayer.

He had never been free from the subtle attacks of evil, though he had decisively defeated the tempter after his baptism. Again and again it was suggested to him that he might win all the kingdoms of this world simply by falling down to pay homage to Satan. What did the method matter compared with the final end? He could rule as he pleased! For many weeks Jesus had faced the meaning of the opposition for his own future. Did it involve, as obedience had involved for prophets before him, sorrow and rejection? Could the Father really conquer through the failure of the Son? He remembered how in Isaiah the Servant of the Lord had endured shame and spitting, but had affirmed his confidence: "Behold, the Lord God will help me; therefore shall I not be confounded; therefore have I set my face as a flint and I know that I shall not be ashamed!" He, too, the Son who was Messiah, must be ready for the same sort of treatment. He recalled the psalmist's joy, after he had gone through experiences of darkness and fear: "Thou preparest a table before me in the presence of mine enemies: thou anointest my head with oil; my cup runneth over." He, too, servant of the Father, had never known the Father to fail him; his head and feet had been literally anointed by a loving, penitent woman; whatever came, his table would be set and he must eat what the Father provided. So did Jesus wrestle with his destiny as a Messiah who had to be in all respects the Son and the Servant of God. And now he would initiate these friends of his into this secret, teaching them what their Messiah must do.

"Tell me," he said to them at the campfire, "who do people say that I am?"

"Some say you are another Baptist."

"Some say you are another Elijah."

"Some say you are a prophet, perhaps the prophet of whom Moses spoke, that God would raise up in the stead of Moses."

"I see," said Jesus. "Now tell me this. Who do you say yourselves that I am?"

Simon, the son of Jonas, was their instant spokesman. "You," he cried, "you are the Messiah of God, the King of Israel!"

Jesus was filled with great joy that these men whom he had chosen still believed in his great glory and majesty. They might not understand all that was involved, but they loved him and honored him. In exultation and ecstasy he gave thanks to the Heavenly Father: "I thank thee, Father, Lord of heaven and earth, that thou hast hidden these things from the wise and understanding, and revealed them to little children. For this, Father, was thy gracious will. All things have been delivered to me by my Father; and no one knows who the Son is except the Father, or who the Father is except the Son and anyone to whom the Son chooses to reveal him."

Thereafter Jesus began to teach them an unexpected truth.

"You are the men whom I have chosen to be with me and to serve with me in proclaiming the Kingdom. Blessed are the eyes that see what you see! For indeed, as you say, I am the King-Messiah on earth, the Anointed of my Father. I tell you, many prophets and kings of old longed to see what you are seeing and to hear what you are hearing, and did not.

"Simon, it is from my Father that you have learned who I am, for he alone can reveal it. You therefore are his choice foundation stone upon which I must build. Do you understand? From now on I shall not call you Simon; you are the man of rock on whom I depend. Your name is Peter!"

"Lord," stammered Peter, "I am not worthy. I am not fit to go forward in the train of the King-Messiah who will overcome the enemies of God."

"I see that you do not really understand," answered Jesus. "Peter . . . all of you . . . listen to me. It is not as you think. I shall not go forward in a blaze of glory to defeat these enemies of whom Peter speaks. Ahead of me are suffering and shame. Ahead is defeat as men reckon defeat. For the Son of Man will be rejected by the priests and leaders of Israel, and they will put him to death!"

Peter started up in amazement, and all of them shrank back in terror. "But, Lord," Peter began, "this cannot be! Is this how the King-Messiah faces the conquest of his Kingdom? Why, this sounds like blasphemy. You must go forward in the power and name of the Almighty. Are you not that Strong One who was to come? Have we not seen your deeds of power? You must go forward. . . ."

Jesus interrupted him angrily. "Stop, Peter! You do not know what you are saying; this is devil's talk and you speak like a servant of Satan. Get you behind me, Satan!"

Then he gathered the troubled, fearful men together into the shelter of his presence and tried to help them to understand the new kind of Messiah whom they served, the Father's Messiah.

"O Peter, Peter, and all of you, my dear children! You must try to understand that my Kingdom is not like the kingdoms of this world at all, where tyrants dominate the lives of their subjects and acknowledge no law but their own wills. My Father rules in love, and in his name I call you and all our nation to the obedience of brotherly love. I have come to look for the lost and to save the sinful from their folly, as you, Levi, were saved from greed. True sovereignty means caring for others, and this lesson I have learned from the Father.

"The Son of Man must care for the lost sheep of the house of Israel. If need be, he must give his life as a ransom for many. For this is an evil generation. Woe to you, Chorazin! Woe to you, Bethsaida! For if the mighty works done in you had been done in Tyre and Sidon, they would have repented long ago, sitting in sackcloth and ashes. As for you, O Capernaum, will you be exalted to heaven? You shall be brought down to hell!

"I warn you, my friends," he went on, "beware of the Herodians and the Pharisees. Woe to them that tithe mint, rue, and all the herbs, yet neglect justice and the love of God! Woe to them that love the front seats at synagogue and the flattery of men in the market place; for they are like graves that men stumble over in the dark! The lawyers have taken away the key of knowledge, so that they neither go in themselves nor let in those who would enter. They add burden to burden on the weak and ignorant among God's people, till the very law of God breaks their backs. Woe to them, for they it is who build tombs for the prophets of God and consent to the deeds of their fathers who slew the prophets! Amen, I tell you, the blood of all the prophets will be required of this generation, for it is evil."

"What then are we to do, Lord?" asked one of the disciples.

"If any man would follow me, he must deny himself. If a man would save his life, he must lose it. What profit is it, if a man win the whole world but lose his own soul?"

Thomas ventured to say, "Master, we have left all . . ."

Jesus continued: "I tell you again and again: Seek first the Kingdom of God and his righteousness. Have faith in the Heavenly Father: pray constantly to the Father. Consider the ravens; they neither sow nor reap, they have neither storehouse nor barn; and yet the Heavenly Father feeds them. Of how much more value are you than the birds! Hear this story:

"The land of a wealthy man brought forth richly; so he thought to himself, 'What shall I do, for I have nowhere to store my crops?' and he said: 'This is what I will do. I will pull down my barns and build larger ones, and there I will store my grain and all my goods. Then will I say to my soul: "Soul, eat and drink and be merry!"' But God said to him: 'Fool! this night your soul is required of you. As for the things you have prepared, whose will they be?'"

With such teaching Jesus tried to guide his disciples at that crucial time, but there was much that they could not take in and he knew he would have to persevere with them throughout the weeks and months that lay ahead. He had chosen them to be with him, and he wanted them to remain loyal to the end.

It was the season for the Festival of Tents when the Jews celebrated the harvest thanksgiving. About a week after Jesus had given to the disciples the strange new messages concerning the Kingdom and his own destiny, a momentous experience befell Peter, James, and John, the three closest to the Master. They went one day with Jesus to Mt. Hermon and there he taught them further about the way that lay ahead and about the fulfillment in himself of all that Moses and the prophets had expected. After a long evening of talk he took them up the mountain for a night of prayer.

"We were tired men, I can tell you," Peter told the others long afterward, "but in the dawning of the new day we saw the Lord stand before us absolutely transfigured with an unearthly glory. His clothes sparkled whiter than usual and there was radiance all about him. It seemed to us that he was still engaged in deep prayerful communion with God and that we with him were caught up into heavenly places.

There he was talking with Moses the Lawgiver of Israel and with Elijah the prophet who was to come and prepare the way for Messiah. He was speaking to them of another exodus and deliverance of God's people which he would himself accomplish at Jerusalem. Oh, it was an eerie and supernatural scene and we were sore afraid! I remember how I stuttered out something to the effect that it was good for us to be there. 'Let us stay on this mount of vision,' I said. 'Let me put up three tents, one for you, one for Moses, and one for Elijah, so that we may keep the festival of thanksgiving with the holy ones.' Then I heard as it were a voice from the sky whispering in my heart: 'No one knows the Father except the Son and anyone to whom the Son chooses to reveal him; and no one but the Father knows who the Son is. This is my Son! Listen to him!' And suddenly the vision was gone and there was Jesus alone with us.

"On the way down we asked him, 'Why is it said that Elijah must first come and then the Messiah?' Jesus answered us: 'Elijah has indeed come, and they have done with him what they pleased, even as it is written. Is it not also written of the Son of Man that he must suffer?' We were quite perplexed, but did not dare to question him further. Later, of course, we understood that he had spoken about John the Baptist and of himself as the Servant of the Lord who should fulfill the prophecies of Isaiah."

Meantime the other disciples had moved southward, and when Jesus and the three had caught up with them, they found that a crowd had gathered round a father and a son, while some scribes were arguing in excited fashion. As soon as Jesus was observed the people rushed to him. "What is going on?" Jesus asked. Then the boy's father called out, "Rabbi, I asked your disciples to expel the evil spirit that haunts my poor lad; he can neither speak nor hear, and whenever he has a seizure he is dashed to the ground, foaming at the mouth and grinding his teeth like a wild beast; then he lies rigid." "O generation of little faith," groaned Jesus, "how long must I put up with this sort of thing? Bring the boy to me." When they did so, the child had a convulsion. "He has been like this since infancy," said the father. "Oh, if you can, have pity on us and help us!" Jesus smiled ruefully. " 'If you can'! Anything is possible for faith." At once the man cried: "But I do believe! Help my unbelief!" Jesus therefore commanded the demon to leave the boy, who was lying rigid on the ground like a corpse. Jesus lifted him by the hand and gave him over to his father's care.

After this he returned to Capernaum, but secretly lest it come to the ears of his enemies. In the house he turned to the disciples and asked, "What were you talking about on the road today?" They were tongue-tied and conscience-stricken, for they had been discussing the coming Kingdom of the Messiah and who should be great in it.

"We'll be going up soon to Jerusalem—it stands to reason we will," declared Simon the Zealot. "The Master must drive out the Romans now by using his wonderful powers, and then he will establish himself in the palace of Pilate. Think of it! All we want to eat and drink; priests to put in their place; governors to appoint for Perea and Galilee; commanders to name for the conquest of other lands!"

"Ha! Wouldn't the Herods and Pilate like to hear that kind of talk, Simon," laughed Judas Iscariot.

"Perhaps so," retorted John, the son of Zebedee, "but would our Master like to hear it? Is this what he has been trying to teach us all these last weeks?"

"You're a hypocrite, John!" said Simon angrily. "Don't think you can get away with it. We know you and your precious brother. We know that with Simon Peter you want the places of honor for yourselves. I have heard you myself, and before now you have hinted as much to the Master, haven't you?"

And because Simon spoke the truth, John had to hold his tongue.

Jesus was displeased and vexed. "Oh, you will all have places of distinction in the Kingdom! Of course you will. You twelve can sit on thrones to judge the tribes of Israel!

"Slow of heart and slow of wit, will you ever learn?" He brought a small boy into their midst and continued: "Look at this little child. Of such is the Kingdom of God! If anyone wants to be first, let him take the last place and become the servant of all. You are not to be called rabbis or teachers, for you have but one Teacher and all of you are brothers. You are to call no man 'father' on earth, for you have but one Father, he who is in heaven, and you are all his children. And do not be called 'masters,' for you have but one Master. Whoever exalts himself shall be humbled, and whoever humbles himself shall be exalted."

While he was in Capernaum some friendly Pharisees came to him with the warning, "Get away from here, for Herod wants to kill you." Jesus told them: "Go and tell that fox I am casting out evil spirits and healing sick men one day and another, but on the third day I must finish my work. One day and another I must be on my way, and the day after that too, for it cannot be that a prophet should be killed outside of Jerusalem."

To the troubled disciples he told this parable:

"A man had a fig tree planted in his vineyard. He came looking for fruit but found none. Next year and a third he came, but there was never any fruit. So he said to his gardener: 'Look, for three years now I have come looking for fruit from this fig tree and I find none. Cut it down; why should it waste good ground?' Then the gardener replied: 'Sir, let it be this year also; let me dig all around it and put in manure. If it bear fruit next year, well and good; but if not, then cut it down.'

"It is the last chance for this nation; don't you understand?" Jesus said to the disciples. "You have heard me tell the people: 'Read the signs of the times. You see a cloud in the western sky and you forecast a shower of rain; and you are quite right. When the stormy desert wind blows from the south, you forecast blistering heat; and you are quite right. If then you know how to read the signs of earth and sky, why cannot you read the signs of this age?' As for you, my men, you have seen the mighty works of God and heard his gracious word, for the Kingdom of God is here and men may enter it by following me.

"Yes, we are going to Jerusalem, for there only can the Son of Man finish the work his Father gave him to do. We shall arrive in time for the next Passover and I shall arrange with my friends in the city to have a room prepared. We are going to sound again the great good news of the Kingdom and to call the people and their leaders to repent and welcome God. It is clear that we shall have no easy passage, for there are enemies who lie in wait to arrest us. Nevertheless the Son of Man goes as it is written of him. In my work the Father will make a new covenant with his people, binding them to himself in love and pardoning all their offenses."

And then there burst from him a cry of anguish, of mingled longing and grief: "O Jerusalem, Jerusalem, that killest the prophets of God and stonest those who are sent to thee! How often would I have gathered thy children together as a hen gathers her brood under her wings, and they would not have me! See, thy House of God lies forsaken! I tell thee, thou shalt not see me again until the day when they say, 'Blessed is he who comes in the name of the Lord!'

"Arise, let us go forth to meet them!"

The Way to Jerusalem

8 THE COMPANY that set out for the south consisted of
   Jesus and his disciples and certain women who were to
care for their needs. These women included Salome and two
Marys: one was Mary of Magdala and the other was the
mother of James and of Joses, all friends of the Lord. They
were leaving old familiar scenes and, in most cases, their
homes on the great adventure of the Kingdom.

Varied hopes and fears mingled in the hearts of the disciples, for, despite all that they had heard, most of them
hoped that somehow, in Jerusalem, God would establish
his rule once and for all; then their Lord would be indeed
a king and a new age would begin. It might be true that
this would require suffering; they understood that. Great
causes demand sacrifices. Victories call for bloodshed. Not
in a day, nor without such effort and trial, would they all
come to the desired end. But they could face that, if the end
was to be as glorious as they imagined! And yet, one or two
did feel depressed and doubtful; the words of Jesus had
struck terror and foreboding into them. In vain Simon the
Zealot tried to laugh away their anxiety: "At any rate he is
going up to his capital," said Simon. "Yes," added Judas
Iscariot, "he has friends there and has plans already made.
Do not doubt. He must put his enemies to flight and reign!"

Where the men stumbled along in divided counsel—awestruck, afraid, or bold—Jesus marched fearlessly and resolutely. He had counted the cost and was ready to pay, so
long as the Father upheld him. His face, tanned in the sun
and the wind, was lifted up toward heaven in faith. His
hands, the firm, skilled hands of a carpenter but also very
tender and sensitive, were an index of his mind and heart.
In his eyes shone the light of heaven, and he strode forward,
imperial with the majesty of God. Following after, the disciples caught their breath in wonder at him.

Early on their journey a young man of winsome appearance ran up and knelt before Jesus. "Good Rabbi," he said,
"what must I do to inherit the eternal life of God's Kingdom?" The reply was brusque and disconcerting. "Good?"
answered Jesus. "Why do you use that word 'good'? There
is no one good but God. You know the Commandments in
the law . . . ." "Rabbi," the youth pleaded eagerly, "all of
them I have kept from my boyhood." Jesus looked at him

lovingly and knew what was in him. "Yes, but there is just one thing still that you lack," he said, with an eye on the rich clothing of the lad. The other's face lighted up as he waited to hear what he must do. "Sell everything that you own and come, follow me!" The light died, his face fell, and slowly he turned away. For he had large possessions and he hadn't bargained for this.

With equal sorrow Jesus watched him go, a recruit who could not follow the Messiah on this road. To his disciples he said: "You see what it is to be burdened with this world's goods and to serve mammon rather than God! There was a rich man once who was clothed in purple and fine linen; he fed richly too every day of his life. At his gate lay a poor beggar called Lazarus, who was so full of sores that the village dogs came and licked them. All that Lazarus wanted in life was to be fed the crumbs that fell from the rich man's table.

"By and by the beggar died and was carried by the angels up to Abraham's bosom. The rich man also died, and was buried. In hell he lifted up his eyes and saw Lazarus afar off in paradise. Then he called out, 'Father Abraham, please have pity on me and send Lazarus to dip his finger in water and to cool my tongue, for I am in anguish in this heat.' Abraham gave him no comfort. 'Son, remember that in your lifetime you had your good things; Lazarus here got only evil. In any case, there is a great gulf between us that none may cross.' The rich man made another request: 'Then I beseech you, Father, send him to my father's house on earth to warn my five brothers there, lest they too come to this place of torment.' 'They have Moses and the prophets, haven't they?' replied Abraham. 'Let them listen to them.' 'No, Father Abraham, they don't listen. But if one were to go to them from the dead, they might repent.' 'Ah,' sighed Abraham, 'I'm afraid that if they won't pay any attention to Moses and the prophets in the Scriptures, they will not be persuaded even if one should rise from the dead!'

"It is virtually impossible," continued Jesus, "for a rich man to enter into the Kingdom." With a smile he added, "Indeed it is easier for a camel to pass through the eye of a needle than for a rich man to get into the Kingdom of God!"

The listeners were absolutely astounded. "Who, then, can get in?" "All things are possible with God," he told them. "Are not you yourselves committed to God?"

By this time they had skirted Samaria, and had crossed Jordan again into Perea. They had now to be ever watchful for spies of Herod and possible ambush.

At the ford of Jordan below Jericho, when they stopped because people had come out to hear Jesus teach, a knotty question about divorce was put to Jesus. It was a trap, for his reputation had gone before him as one who had dared to challenge the traditions of the most notable religious leaders. What would the Galilean have to say about this one?

"Is it ever lawful for a man to divorce his wife?"

"What does the law of Moses say?"

"Moses allows it," they answered.

"Truly he did," agreed Jesus, "but it was only because men are so hardhearted. In the book of Genesis we read, 'God made them male and female,' and you would accept that as coming from Moses too, wouldn't you?" They nodded assent.

"Well, it goes on to say that 'for this reason a man shall leave his father and mother and be joined to his wife, and these two shall become one flesh.' So a married couple are in fact one, not two. Therefore, what God has joined together let not man put asunder!"

They were quite dumfounded. Moses had contradicted Moses! Why, this would mean that a husband was tied to his wife till she died, for only by death did God break their bond. Jesus smiled at their bewilderment, knowing perfectly well that he must be still more explicit. "You see, friends, a wife is bound to her husband too, till he dies. There is only one law for man and woman. That is why it is adultery committed against his wife for a man to divorce her and to marry another."

There it was! No one else had ever told them that a woman had equal standing before God in the marriage relationship. What else might he say? . . . They did not wait to find out.

There were men on that road to Jerusalem who thought they would like to join Jesus. When one of them said blithely, "I'll follow you wherever you go," Jesus wondered if the man knew the cost. "Foxes have holes and the birds of the air have nests," he told him, "but the Son of Man is homeless." To another who wanted to take time out to say good-by to his friends at home Jesus said, "No man who puts his hand to the plow and looks back is fit for the Kingdom of God." It was stern doctrine. Once Jesus met one whom he desired for his service. "Follow me!" said Jesus. But the man excused himself. "Let me go home first to arrange for my old father's funeral." Jesus gave him no quarter at all. "Let the dead bury their own dead! You go and proclaim far and wide that the Kingdom of God is at men's doors."

Stern and harsh the conditions might seem, but Jesus was on a road that led him, he knew well, to rejection and death. In such circumstances he must challenge only the best and the highest in men. "If anyone comes to me and does not 'hate' his parents, his wife and children, yes, even his own life, he cannot be my disciple. It is all or nothing now! What king would dare to make war with ten thousand against

another who had twenty thousand men? Would he not send
a herald and ask for terms? Count the cost! for unless a man
will hazard everything, he cannot follow me on this road."

Having recrossed Jordan, they approached Jericho.

In the warm spring sunshine more people came to see
and hear him, and a lawyer stood forth and tested him.

"Sir, what should I do to inherit eternal life?"

"You are a lawyer. What does it say in the law of God?"

" 'Thou shalt love the Lord thy God with all thy heart
and with all thy soul and with all thy strength and with all
thy mind. Again, thou shalt love thy neighbor as thyself.' "

"Quite right," said Jesus. "Do that, and you will live."

The lawyer began to justify himself. He wanted more
than quotations from the book. He would draw this teacher
out!

"But, Rabbi, the question is, Who is my neighbor?"

In reply Jesus told him a story:

"A certain man went down from Jerusalem to Jericho.
He fell among thieves who stripped him of his clothes,
wounded him, and left him half-dead. By chance there came
down a priest that way; but when he saw the man, he passed
by on the other side. Likewise a Levite came down. When
he reached the spot, he crossed and looked at the poor fellow, but passed by on the other side. Then a certain Samaritan, on his journey, came to the place; and when he saw the
man he had compassion on him. He bound up his wounds,
pouring in oil and wine; he set him on his own beast and
brought him to an inn and took care of him. The next day,
when he departed, he took out some money and gave it to
the innkeeper. 'Take care of him,' said the Samaritan, 'and
if you have to spend more than this, I will give it to you
when I return.' "

Jesus looked at the lawyer. "Which one acted as neighbor
to the man who fell among thieves?"

"He that showed mercy to him," the lawyer said.

"Go and do likewise!" said Jesus.

Farther up that same road a little man had climbed a tree, the better to see what went on. His name was Zacchaeus and he was a leading tax collector, a man of some wealth and many enemies. He had been much excited at the prospect of seeing this man from Nazareth of whom so many things were said or whispered. He had friends who were friends of people who knew Levi of Capernaum, a man of much the same sort of occupation as Zacchaeus.

But so dense was the crowd, so undersized the little fellow and so unpopular, that he could not get near Jesus and his company at all. He had therefore run farther up the street and climbed a sycamore tree which gave him a perfect view. He didn't know that he had made himself quite conspicuous and that voices called out his name in derision as the procession moved along. Then Jesus reached the spot and, to the amazement of everyone, halted and looked up with a smile. "Zacchaeus," he said, "come down quickly, for I'd like to spend the evening in your home, if I may." In a flash the tax collector was down that tree and giving Jesus the warmest of welcomes. He was himself overcome with mingled joy and shame, for he seemed to know at once in the presence of Jesus that he was a sinner. The wonderful thing was that with this knowledge the kindness of Jesus had also brought the certainty that he was loved. What a difference that made to the man! At the door of his home he stopped, saying, "Sir, the half of my goods I give to the poor; if I have cheated anyone, I restore it fourfold." Jesus was absolutely delighted, because this was how the coming of God's Kingdom turned a man's life right side up. "This day," he told them, "the life of salvation has come to this house; this man too is a genuine son of Abraham!"

All that some of the citizens of half-pagan Jericho could

mutter was: "Just think of it! The prophet has gone off to be the guest of a rascal—it beats all!"

On the way out of Jericho next day there was a blind beggar at the roadside. When he heard that it was Jesus of Nazareth who was passing by his stall, he shouted: "Son of David! Jesus, Son of David, have pity on me!" People told him to be quiet and not to trouble the rabbi, but he went on calling: "Son of David! Jesus, have pity on me!" It might not have mattered so much if he hadn't persisted in using these words about the Son of David, for this seemed to mean that he thought Jesus was the long-expected prince of the line of King David; that the Messiah, in fact, was passing his way, and he was determined to get some share of the good things this new king was supposed to bring.

The commotion and the cries came to the attention of Jesus and he ordered the man to be brought to him. "What is your name?" "I am Bartimaeus." "What do you want me to do for you, Bartimaeus?" "Sir," said the beggar, "let me have my sight." Jesus was moved by the man's belief that he could help him. "Your faith is your salvation," he told him. "Yes, you can see; go your way." Bartimaeus opened his eyes and shouted for joy. From that hour he followed Jesus on the road to Jerusalem; for Bartimaeus the new age had arrived.

The Road to the Cross

9 EXCITEMENT gripped the crowd on the journey toward the Holy City. They had seen and heard wonders; they were going to see the house of God in all its splendor and join in the happy Passover festivities. Some among them had come far on pilgrimage to Palestine, on the journey of a lifetime of saving, of planning, of expectation. These Jewish strangers from distant lands knew little of what had

been going on in the land, the life and death of John the Baptist and now the ministry of Jesus. They got rather a shock at hearing the title "Son of David" and they wanted to know, "Who, then, is this prophet on his way with a band of followers to the capital?" Others in the crowd were Galileans who knew the great hopes that had been entertained of Jesus; it was still possible, so far as they knew, that Jesus would turn out to be the Messiah. Up and down the fifteen miles between Jericho and Jerusalem ran all kinds of rumors about Jesus—a teacher who taught as none other did: of a leper healed, a maiden raised from death, a wild man out of whom a whole legion of evil spirits had been cast; of the multitude that were fed in the desert and thought they were already feasting in the Kingdom of God. Voices whispered that Herod feared this new prophet, that the priests and Pharisees had investigated him, and that Jesus had consistently got the better of disputes with the scribes about the interpretation of the law of God.

A week before Passover, Jesus and his friends reached the village of Bethany and resolved to stay there for the Sabbath. The disciples were told to make their way inconspicuously to the house of two sisters, Mary and Martha, who had a large house where they could all stay.

The sisters gave them an affectionate welcome, and at once Martha set about the business of their entertainment. Mary sat with Jesus while his feet were washed and he received refreshment after the dust and heat of the road. Jesus talked to her about the life of God's Kingdom and answered her questions, for she was devoted to his purpose. Poor Martha fretted over the household duties: so many guests, and servants who would not always jump to do her bidding. Finally she came to Jesus with a complaint: "Do you think it fair that my sister should leave me to attend to everything by myself? Tell her to help me." But Jesus laughed. "O Martha, my dear, you're so anxious and bothered about many things! Only one thing really counts and Mary has chosen it. It shall not be taken from her." Martha felt the rebuke in the gentle voice and wasn't sure that she quite understood what he meant.

After the Sabbath was ended two of the disciples were detailed to slip into the outskirts of Jerusalem to a street where a colt would be found tied. All had been arranged, and Jesus gave them the code. "A man will say to you, 'Why are you loosing the colt?' and you will reply, 'The Master needs it and will send it back speedily.' Bring it then to the Mount of Olives, for I will enter Jerusalem from that direction."

Everything took place as he had planned, and on the morning of the first day of the week, Jesus rode into the Holy City from the Mount of Olives. The company of disciples were caught up in a vast crowd of pilgrims who were chanting one of the psalms as they marched, full of excitement the nearer they came to the gates of Jerusalem. This is what they sang:

"Blessed be the name of the Lord from this time forth and for evermore! . . . The Lord hath been mindful of us: he will bless us; he will bless the house of Israel; he will bless the house of Aaron. . . . O Lord, truly I am thy servant; I am thy servant and the son of thine handmaid; thou hast loosed my bonds. I will offer to thee the sacrifice of thanksgiving, and will call upon the name of the Lord. I will pay my vows unto the Lord now in the presence of all his people, in the courts of the Lord's house, in the midst of thee, O Jerusalem. Praise ye the Lord!"

There was singing and dancing, and laughter and joy in all their faces; and Jesus entered into their joyfulness, for he too had come to give thanks to his Father. He was thinking of the marvelous deliverance at Passover time in Egypt centuries before and of the covenant between God and his people that had followed. He was thinking also of the deliverance from blindness, fear, hate, and self-righteousness that he hoped still to achieve in the spirit of the Father; but he was ready for whatever suffering this might demand of him before God could make a new and more wonderful covenant of love with his people. So he and his disciples chanted the psalm of the pilgrim way amid the tumult:

"O give thanks unto the Lord, for he is good; because his mercy endures forever. . . . The Lord is on my side; I shall not fear; what can man do to me? . . . The right hand of the Lord is exalted; the right hand of the Lord acts valiantly. I shall not die, but live and declare the works of the Lord. . . . Open to me the gates of righteousness; I will go into them, and I will praise the Lord."

Amen! thought Jesus the Son of Man, even though I die, I come to you as your King, in the name of your God! Will you lift up your eyes and see your King in his glory, fulfilling the ancient prophecy of Zechariah? "Rejoice greatly, O daughter of Zion; shout, O daughter of Jerusalem. Behold, thy King cometh unto thee. He is just and bringeth salvation. He is meek and mounted on a donkey, even on a colt, the foal of a donkey." So will I go into your gates: open them unto me, and let us praise the Lord!

The citizens of Jerusalem, accustomed though they were to bands of pilgrims and singing at Passover time, were drawn to see why there was such an unexpectedly large crowd and such happiness. To one of the Galileans they said: "What's the meaning of this? Who is this that goes up with such singing and acclamation?" "Don't you know?" was the answer. "This is our prophet from Galilee, Jesus of Nazareth."

On they went singing, into the outer courts of the house of God:

"I will praise thee; for thou hast heard me, and art become my salvation. The stone which the builders rejected has become the headstone of the corner; it is the Lord's doing and it is marvelous in our eyes. . . .

"This is the day which the Lord hath made; we will rejoice and be glad in it."

At this point the signal was always given for pilgrims and citizens to wave their lulab branches with exultation, as they remembered God's loving-kindness to their forefathers in Egypt. As the people chanted, "Save now, I beseech thee, O Lord; O Lord, I beseech thee, send now prosperity," they waved their branches and jostled round the colt on which Jesus was riding. They made him the focus of their joy, some knowing nothing of what it was they did, some welcoming him because of rumor, the Galileans because he was their prophet and they wanted so much the coming of a kingdom in which he might reign. Thus, as he had foretold, Jesus returned to Jerusalem to the accompaniment of the words that followed in the psalm:

"Blessed be he that cometh in the name of the Lord!" Now the disciples themselves shouted: "Hosanna! Blessed be the kingdom of our father David! Hosanna in the highest!"

There were as usual Pharisees in the Temple courts; and the coincidence of this singing and acclamation with Jesus' arrival made them shudder, for they read in it his own shameless avowal of Messiahship. "Rabbi," they cried, "rebuke your disciples." All that he would say to them was, "I tell you, if they were silent, the very stones would cry out!"

It was getting late and his company were overexcited.

Jesus therefore took time only to look at what was going on in the Temple, and then withdrew to Bethany to spend the night.

But the religious leaders conferred together, genuinely afraid that Jesus had come up to the Passover to claim a kingdom. They knew the symbolism of the feast as well as he did. And they had already resolved that he would never win a kingdom. They had writhed under the criticisms of their teaching; they distrusted his right to teach; they saw none of the signs of a Messiah that they had been led to expect or that they wanted. The man was dangerous. What would he do on the morrow?

The next day as he came from Bethany, Jesus halted by the wayside to look at the city spread out before him, set on a hill, gathering into itself the whole history of his nation. If it rejected him, if the hotheads once started a rebellion, as they were quite sure to do, its fate was forewritten and inescapable. A great cry burst from him: "O Jerusalem, Jerusalem, would that even today thou knewest the things that make for thy peace! But as it is they are hidden from thine eyes. Days will come when thine enemies will surround thee and besiege thee and hem thee in on every side. They will raze thee to the ground and thy children too, leaving not one stone upon another; for thou hast not known the judgment and the opportunity that have overtaken thee or who it is that comes to thee!" And Jesus wept over Jerusalem.

Once inside the walls he made straight for the Temple, the holy place where the nation centered its worship of God. Yesterday in the Court of the Gentiles he had seen the bustle of men driving into its courtyards the sacrificial animals, and solemn rabbis clustered in groups arguing about him, the Father's Son. Yesterday he had heard the shouts of pilgrims and the clink of the coins at the exchangers' tables where they had paid their dues in foreign currency. And his heart was sick once more at the commercialism of it all. Here, where alone the Gentiles were permitted to draw near to Israel's God within the Temple of Jerusalem, the priests had turned a place of prayer into a brawling market. Months before, Jesus had put away the temptation to reform this place by spectacular methods; but he still had authority to teach Israel how to worship. Away with these babbling tongues and these fences to keep out the poor and the foreigner! With contempt and holy wrath he strode over and upset the tables of the financiers; then he turned to the stall of the pigeons and drove out the merchants; he would not let the traders drive their sheep and oxen through the Temple courts, but stood there, eyes flashing, in all the majesty of his holy life and all the assurance of his divine commission. He was about his business in his Father's house! If he had to die for it, he had struck a blow for holiness. He had defied the Temple police and the agelong line of the priesthood. Now the gauntlet was down and the refiner's fire was aflame. He had come suddenly to the Temple and done his great deed in the holiest place in his capital. Men shrank back from him in terror; not a hand was lifted to stop him; none dared to say him nay. Never had they seen anything like this! Never had man spoken as this man! "Look!" he called across the court, "is it not written in the Scripture: 'My house shall be called a house of prayer for all the nations'? You have made it a den of robbers!"

When the priests and teachers got their breath back, they challenged him. "By what authority are you doing this?"

Jesus knew the test, but he would catch them in their own net. "I will tell you, if you will answer one question: 'Was the baptism of John from God or from man?'"

That put them in a quandary. To say "from man" was to

assert that John was an impostor, but many people believed that he was a true prophet. To say "from God" was to lay themselves open to the next move by Jesus: "Why, then, did you not believe and accept him?" Jesus would make at least the same claim for himself: he spoke in God's name. They were caught and they knew it. Very sheepishly they refused to commit themselves and played for time. "We don't know." "I see," said Jesus. "Very well, I will not tell you what my authority is." Let them find out!

As they left the Temple that day, his disciples drew his attention to the massive stones used in its building. Jesus said to them: "There will not be left one stone upon another. It will all be destroyed." This saying was overheard by enemies.

When the disciples asked him further about the future, Jesus taught them:

"There will be great tribulations before the Kingdom of my Father is fully triumphant and the Son of Man is glorified. You who believe on me will be scattered like sheep without a shepherd, and you will leave me alone to my fate." There was muttering of dissent. "Yes, you will. You have not understood me and you expect the wrong things. But there will be an end and I shall be vindicated. Just as you know that summer is near when the fig tree puts forth leaves, so you will know that the end is at hand by certain signs. Watch for them, for no one knows the day or the hour. The angels in heaven do not know; the Son of Man does not know; only the Father himself knows. So you do not know when the master of the house will come: in the evening, at midnight, or in the dawning. Watch therefore, lest coming he find you asleep."

On Tuesday he returned to the Temple and taught. Again the religious leaders tried to trap him. "Is it lawful to pay taxes to Caesar?" they asked him. "Bring me a coin," he answered. "Whose likeness is here?" "Caesar's," they said. "Very well, give to Caesar what is Caesar's and give to God what is God's." Once more he had seen through their hypocrisy, and once more his wit had given them a puzzle to think about. Some of them could stand it no longer and made an unsuccessful attempt to arrest him.

But the real initiative lay with Jesus. A scribe came asking, "Which is the first commandment?" and Jesus replied: "It is: 'Hear, O Israel: the Lord our Lord is one Lord. And thou shalt love the Lord thy God with all thy heart and with all thy soul and with all thy mind and with all thy strength.' The second is this, 'Thou shalt love thy neighbor as thyself.'" "Well said, Rabbi," answered the scribe, "for such love is much more than all the burnt offerings and all the sacrifices that are offered in this Temple." Jesus perceived that he had spoken wisely and told him, "You are not far from the Kingdom of God."

Then Jesus put a question of his own. "Why do the scribes keep saying that the Messiah is 'the Son of David'? In the sacred writings David himself says, 'The Lord said to my Lord, Sit at my right hand till I put thine enemies under thy feet.' So David himself calls Messiah 'Lord'; how then can he be his 'Son'?" The people who had come round to listen were intensely interested in this and enjoyed the battle of wits. It was obvious that the official teachers of the law were annoyed by the sharp way Jesus had denounced the popular idea that the Messiah must be an earthly king in the line and likeness of David. What other kind of Messiah might he have in mind?

Jesus went on to tell a parable that seemed to hit at the Pharisees and the Sadducees, the two great parties in the land who were considered to be God's ministers in care of his people. Jesus said: "A man planted a vineyard and rented it to tenants, then departed to another country.

When he sent his servants to collect the fruit of the vineyard in terms of the covenant, the tenants beat them up and sent them back empty-handed; some they even killed. At last the owner decided to send his son, his only son, for, he thought, they will surely respect my son. But those tenants said to one another, 'This is the heir; come, let us kill him too and seize the inheritance for ourselves.' This they did, and cast the body out of the vineyard. What will the owner do? He will come and destroy the tenants and give the vineyard to others."

No one knew better than the teachers of Scripture that the prophets and singers of old had likened Israel to the vineyard of the Lord. This talk about the tenants and the son clearly referred to themselves and Jesus. It was the last straw, and they determined to get rid of him as quickly as possible. "But we must be careful to avoid any riot, for many of the Galilean pilgrims here believe in him, and perhaps others also. We must act swiftly and secretly, and before the Passover festival."

Jesus was well aware of their hostility and withdrew to Bethany. To his friends he confessed: "I have come to set a fire on the earth; would that it were already kindled! I have a baptism with which I must be baptized; how I am hemmed in until it be accomplished! Did you think I would bring peace? No. I tell you, it is division. Families will be divided because of me: father against son, mother against daughter, daughter against her mother, and son against his father."

On Wednesday evening he was invited to supper in the home of a former leper called Simon. While he was there, Mary of Bethany, his friend and disciple, came with an alabaster jar of very costly perfume. She broke the jar and poured the perfume over his head, so that the room was filled with the fragrance. Amid mutterings in the gathering

Judas Iscariot said, "She might have sold it for a large sum and given the money to the poor; this is sheer waste." Jesus, however, spoke up sharply in her defense: "Let her alone and do not trouble her. For she has done a beautiful thing to me. You have the poor with you always, Judas, but you will not have me with you always. She has done her best. She has anointed my body in advance for its burial. Amen, I tell you, this that she has done will be remembered and told wherever my story is told, for her memorial."

Judas was angry at this public rebuke. He realized now that Jesus was preparing himself to die. His purpose was not, after all, to fight the enemies of their nation. Judas would no longer serve such a Messiah! In the night, therefore, he slipped out and went to the chief priests. "How much is information worth that will enable you to arrest my Master Jesus? He is my Master no more." "Thirty pieces of silver," they said eagerly. "Done!" said Judas. "He goes out often in the evening to the gardens below the Mount of Olives. I will find out his plans and let you have word when you may safely take him." And the chief priests for their part made preparations and sent for the witnesses who would testify that Jesus had sworn to lay the Temple of God in ruins.

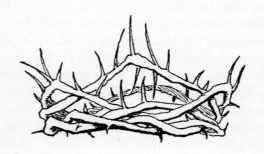

The Lord in All His Glory

10 JESUS KNEW that Judas had deserted him; he could never be deceived. This meant that the decisive hour was at hand; his enemies could not afford to wait. If they were to get him out of the way before the festival and the high Sabbath following, they must strike at him immediately.

On the Thursday of that momentous week he knew what

his own reaction would have to be; he would celebrate this Passover in the only way left to him, by binding the rest of the disciples into a covenant with the Father in the ritual of their farewell meal together. "Go into the city," he told two of them, when he had made his plans. "A man will meet you, and you will know him because he will be carrying a water jar on his head. He will take you to a house where you will give this sign to the householder: 'The rabbi says, "Where is the room where I am to celebrate the Passover with my disciples?"' Then he will show you a large, furnished upper room. Make everything ready there for us."

Judas came back and rejoined the others as though nothing had happened; he had to find out where Jesus meant to spend the night.

The same evening after dark, because of the plotters, Jesus brought the Twelve to the upper room and there they had supper. During the meal he rose, tied back his robe, and prepared a basin of water. Then, with a towel about his arm, he washed the disciples' feet and wiped them with the towel. Peter was astonished and drew back. "Lord, are you washing my feet?" he cried. "Yes, Peter; afterward you will understand." "Never! I cannot allow you to wash my feet, for I am your servant." "Peter, Peter, unless I cleanse you, you cannot belong to me; though indeed you will not all be clean, even so." Then said Peter, "Wash not my feet only, but also my hands and my head!" Jesus told him that it was enough to wash his feet. "You call me Master and Teacher, and you do well. If, then, I, your Master and Teacher, have washed your feet, you must do the same also for one another. I have chosen you, and yet one of you is a traitor."

"What did he say?" they asked one another when they heard these words. "What does he mean?" And, "Lord, is it I?" they said to him. Jesus dipped a morsel in a dish and gave it to Judas. "Go quickly," he said to him; "do whatever you must." And Judas went out into the darkness. The other disciples did not know why Judas had left.

Jesus took a loaf and gave thanks to the Father for all his goodness and tender mercy. Next he broke the bread and divided it among them. "Take, eat; this means my body which is broken for you. Do this in remembrance of me." The men were awe-struck by the words and did not realize what it all involved. After supper Jesus took a cup and gave them wine to drink from it as a brotherhood. "This means that in my blood God is about to make effective a new covenant of love with his people. Drink often of it in memory of me."

The disciples did as he commanded them, but they were bewildered men. "O how I longed to eat Passover with you all this year, and I may not!" Jesus went on. "Never again shall I drink of the fruit of the vine till I drink it new in the Kingdom of my Father. Yet I am the true vine and my Father is the gardener; you are the branches. My Father removes the fruitless branches and prunes the vine so that it may be more fruitful. If you do my will, you will never lose my companionship, your joy will be complete, and the Father will be glorified. In this world you too will have trouble; for if they have called the Master Beelzebul, how much more will they accuse his servants of devilry! I have chosen you and you are mine; I do not call you servants any more, but friends. When the power of my Father's Spirit falls on you, you will give witness to me.

"Peter, I have prayed for you, because the evil one desires to have you. I have prayed for you all, that the Father may keep you from the power of evil. As my Father sent me, so I am sending you; he who receives you receives me. And for your sake I have dedicated myself, so that you too may be consecrated in the truth.

"Now the hour approaches. Arise, and let us go forth to meet what comes!"

When they had sung together one of the psalms, they left the house secretly in the direction of the Mount of Olives, crossed the Brook Kidron, and entered the Garden of Gethsemane. "Stay here," Jesus said to the company. "I am going ahead to pray." He took Peter, James, and John with him, and the burden of his vocation lay heavy upon him. Judas was about to bring his enemies to seize him; his familiar friend would betray him into wicked hands, the hands of the priests of God. Anguish and horror lay before him and bitter grief welled up within him. "I am much distressed," he said to the three men. "I would pray alone to my Father. Wait here and keep watch with me." So there in the dark garden he wrestled with his destiny, sore-tried, tested, and tempted still. Must he go on? Was there absolutely no alternative? "O Abba, Father," the men heard him shout. "O Abba, Father, let this hour pass!" Jesus returned to the three, but they had fallen asleep in their weariness and nervous concern. Again he went beyond them and prayed that the cup of his torment might be taken from him. "Nevertheless not my will, but thine, be done," he prayed. Soon he heard the sound of men approaching from the city. He was worn out by his vigil but sustained by the love of his Father. He roused the sleeping disciples and gathered the whole company. "The hour has come, and the Son of Man is betrayed into the hands of his foes."

Judas appeared, knowing that he would find them here. "There is your man," he told the leader of the police. Then he went up to Jesus and gave him the kiss of friendship; for this was the sign agreed on lest there be any mistake in the dark. The armed men moved in to arrest Jesus. Jesus looked at Judas. "Do you betray me with a kiss?" To the guard he called, "For whom are you looking?" They said, "Jesus of

Nazareth." "I am he." But they fell back before this man who showed no fear, whose face frightened them with its unearthly calm and power. Peter would have interfered to resist, but Jesus commanded him to put away his weapon. "I am Jesus of Nazareth," he repeated to the band brought by Judas. "Each day I have been teaching in the Temple without hindrance. Why have you come out against me as if I were a brigand?" Meanwhile men were moving round to cut off every avenue of escape and his own followers were fearful and restive. "Very well," said Jesus. "Take me." . . . And there was a rush of armed men about him and a tumult of shouting. "But let these men go," he went on, and turned to point out his disciples. But he found that he was alone amid his enemies, for all the disciples had forsaken him and fled.

They brought Jesus in the night to an informal trial before Annas, the father-in-law of the high priest and himself a former high priest. In the meantime Peter and another friend of Jesus, one who knew the high priest and his household, had followed at a safe distance and watched to see where he was taken. With a word to the maidservant at the door, his friend brought Peter into the courtyard, where they mingled with the police guards at a bright open brazier.

Accusers stood up, as arranged, to say that "this man spoke evilly about the house of God," and "threatened to destroy the Temple and to build another not made with hands." Yet the witnesses could not agree on the same form of words, and the law required that there should be adequate agreement before their testimony could be accepted. All this time the prisoner was silent before his accusers. Annas became exasperated by this behavior. "Have you nothing to say for yourself?" he blustered. "Are you the Messiah of Israel?" This was the real charge. Did the

Galilean prophet claim to be the Lord's Anointed, King David's greater Son? If so, what proofs would he offer?

"Are you the Messiah of Israel?" Annas leaned forward to ask, and everyone waited tensely to hear the answer.

"I am the Son of Man," said Jesus, "and you will see the Son of Man at the right hand of my Father in heaven."

Enough! It was enough. "Out of his own mouth he is condemned! What need is there for witnesses? He is a blasphemer; you heard him say that he is the Son of the Father. What is your verdict?" With one accord they pronounced him guilty and deserving to die.

Under their law the penalty for blasphemy was stoning, but the Romans would not let the Jews fulfill a death sentence without their approval. Would Pilate agree? Wouldn't public stoning rouse the multitude and all the friends Jesus might have in the city? There would be a riot, and Rome would never stand for rioting at festival time. There might be a rising and rebellion. So they took counsel together to see what could be done. At any rate, Jesus must die.

In the cold courtyard the maid who had let them in was taking another look at Peter. "Why, you were with that fellow from Nazareth!" But he denied it vehemently. Bravely he stayed by the charcoal fire which the armed men tended, until another accused him. "Haven't I seen you with Jesus of Nazareth?" "You have not, curse you. I don't even know the man!" A little later they were bringing Jesus through the courtyard on the way to his cell. "There he is!" they cried to Peter. "Are you sure you weren't with him in the Garden tonight? You are a Galilean all right, for your accent betrays you." Somewhere in the late night air a cock crew in the expectation of dawn. Jesus turned and looked at Peter; the maid and the armed men looked at them both. There was a moment's pause. "No, no," cried

Peter, "I don't recognize this fellow. I am not one of his," and with oaths and curses he ran from the place. But away from his enemies, safe for a time, Peter broke down and wept bitterly. He was in the power of the evil one and so was his beloved Master. It was like the end of the world.

Early next morning the full council of the Jews assembled, with Caiaphas the high priest presiding. Without more ado they found the prisoner guilty of blasphemy and of claiming to be the King-Messiah of Israel. Then they sought and obtained an audience with Pilate, the Roman governor, and before him they left out the charge of blasphemy; Rome did not care what religious ideas this Jew or that might have contrary to priestly or Pharisaic ideas. "Here is Jesus of Nazareth who claims to be the King of the Jews. We have found him guilty under our law; and by our law he ought to die."

"What has he done?" "Done? Isn't it enough for you that he is a traitor, an enemy of your emperor and a threat to our peace?" Pilate took Jesus and examined him in his own chambers. "So you are a king?" he mocked, looking with scorn at the figure before him. This man did not look as if he could ever have been a menace. But the prisoner did not answer in any weakness or fear. "That is what you say," he said to Pilate, "though others have put it into your head. I am indeed a King, but my Kingdom is not of this world."

The governor returned to report that he had found no crime that could be charged against Jesus. Maddened at the thought that Jesus might escape them, the Jewish leaders protested that they simply wanted his confirmation of a sentence they had already reached. "In any case," they taunted him, "it won't look well if you do not punish Caesar's enemy. You will not be Caesar's friend." Pilate gave in. What was a poor deluded Galilean compared with his own safety and the security of Rome in this Godforsaken land? He washed his hands of the affair, lest worse befall him. "On your own heads be it. Take him away, and have him crucified!"

Crowds of people had gathered, early as it was; and when the prisoner was exhibited to them, condemned and about to be scourged, many voices shouted: "Crucify him! Crucify him!" The chief priests reminded Pilate that the lambs would be slain that afternoon for the Passover sacrifice and the feast in the homes that evening. "We want the crucifixion this afternoon," they told him, "so that nothing will interfere with the evening festivities. We could not answer for the consequences of delay at such a time as this. Some ruffian Galileans might attempt a rescue."

They scourged Jesus till he was bloody and bruised all over. They mocked him, and the soldiers played with him, a flesh-and-blood representation of the make-believe "king" of their Roman holidays. They wove a crown of thorns and clamped it on his brow so that he could hardly see for the streaming blood. Then, dancing round him, after they had blindfolded him, they cried, "Prophesy, O king; tell us who struck you that time!"

Pilate had an inscription carved on wood to be placed above the crosspiece of his cross: "Jesus of Nazareth, the King of the Jews." So he wrote, in all the languages of the land, Latin, Greek, and Aramaic. No complaints from the priests could move him. They could argue till doomsday that he had merely claimed to be king. He would be avenged on these Jews. This was what he would do for them at their own request. He would crucify their king!

Jerusalem was in an uproar, but the Temple police and the garrison troops had the situation well in hand. Crowds lined the road that led from the city to Calvary outside the walls, where the criminals of the day would be strung up to die in the noonday sun. Galilean pilgrims watched in grim silence; aliens from other lands; Jews home on pilgrimage. And here and there among them, following secretly, were the women who had come up with the disciples and Jesus from Capernaum; and Peter, James, John, and the rest.

On the road the condemned Jesus stumbled under the weary weight of the cross, and the centurion of the guard ordered Simon of Cyrene, who had chanced to be on hand just at the time, to carry it. So they brought Jesus to the hill of death, tied to a soldier, worn out with care and scourging and heartbreak. They stripped him of his robe, for which the guards gambled at the foot of the cross; they nailed him by the palms of his hands to the cruelest of wood; and they let him hang there in the heat from noon till three, parched, racked, alone.

His friends were in a state of collapse themselves and could hardly endure the day. But passers-by laughed with the hatred and contempt reserved for the kind of criminal usually put on crosses; and priests called to him, "If you are the Son of the Blessed, come down from the cross and we will believe you!"

Jesus said, "Father, forgive them, for they know not what they do."

Two thieves were being crucified at the same time, one on his left hand, the other on his right. One of them joined in roughly in the insults that were being heaped on Jesus, but the other answered him: "Is there no fear of God at all in you? We have been justly condemned for our misdeeds, but this man is no criminal." Then he spoke to Jesus, "Sir, will you remember me in the day of your glory?" Jesus said, "Today you will be with me in paradise."

As the afternoon went on, people noticed how strangely dark it was, but they little knew that the day was dark because what was being put out was the Light of the world.

Jesus was in agony. "I thirst," he moaned. On a long javelin the rude soldiers passed up a sponge filled with vinegar. In the great darkness a loud cry from the dying man startled the spectators. *"Eli, Eli, lama sabachthani?* My God, my God, why hast thou forsaken me?" Some who heard it shuddered, others mocked, saying: "He is calling for Elijah. Let us wait and see if the prophet Elijah will appear to save him!" But nothing happened, except that Jesus' breath came faster and in gasps. He managed to whisper: "It is finished. I have finished the work." And then they heard him repeat the evening prayer he had learned from his mother: "Father, into thy hands I commend my spirit." And with this prayer he breathed his last.

The Jews had asked that death might be hastened, so that the festival might not be polluted by the corpses. The soldiers, therefore, went from criminal to criminal to break their legs and give them a merciful release; but when they came to Jesus, he was already dead. One of them pierced his side with a spear and there flowed out blood and watery fluid. The centurion of the guard had watched Jesus die and now he saluted him with the words, "Truly this was a god's son."

Joseph of Arimathaea, a secret disciple of Jesus and a member of the Jewish council, went to the governor and requested that he might be permitted to take the body of Jesus down from the cross. Pilate was surprised that death had come so soon, but, on receiving official confirmation, he gave the necessary authority. Joseph brought a linen shroud and wrapped the body in it; then, without the embalming usual at that time because the Sabbath was about to begin, he laid the body in a rock-hewn tomb in a garden that he owned, and rolled a great stone hard against the face of the tomb to seal it. The perfume that Mary of Bethany had broken over her Lord was the only anointing he received for his burial. The two other Marys, Mary of Magdala and Joses' mother, assisted Joseph of Arimathaea in the last, sad, sacred offices of love and saw the place where they laid the body of Jesus.

In the Temple that same afternoon about three, the priests on duty slew the sacrificial lambs and poured the blood over the altar in glad remembrance that once long ago God had delivered Israel from the captivity of Egypt. Their own portion of the meat they kept for the evening festival; the other lambs were given back to the families of the nation who had made ready to celebrate in their homes. Men told afterward how something exceedingly strange had happened about the time of the sacrifice, when Jesus also was hanging in his death throes at Calvary. There was one very special part of the sanctuary into which the high priest only was allowed to go, and that but once a year on the Day of Atonement; there in the very presence of God he confessed the sins of the nation and begged for pardon. This shrine, the Holy of Holies, was curtained off from secular gaze; it reminded God's people that he was a holy God and that the way into his presence was barred against sinners. On this afternoon, in the darkness surrounding the crucifixion, the veil of the Holy of Holies was ripped into two pieces. The secret shrine was exposed! The way into the divine presence lay wide open!

Desolate and hunted, the disciples of Jesus crept dolefully and cautiously back to the meeting place of the night before, the house with a large furnished upper room, the house of young John Mark and his mother. Their minds were quite stunned by the magnitude of their loss, and the incredible pace at which the events of the last week had moved. Peter, who had denied his Master, was inconsolable, and he made no attempt now to excuse himself. Not one of them could bear to think of the future, for every hope had been dashed to the ground. Every effort of Jesus to prepare them for such sorrow and desolation seemed to have been useless; they had not understood what he meant. They had not been loyal to the end. But this was the end! Was life worth living any more?

From Friday at sunset till Saturday evening they kept sorrowful Sabbath.

At dawn on the first day of the week the two Marys took spices and perfumes that they had bought as soon as Sabbath was over. "We are going to the tomb to anoint the body of our beloved Master," they told the others. "It will be perfectly safe; the Temple police won't pay any attention to a couple of simple women, and we know the place."

As they drew near to the garden they said to one another anxiously: "The stone! We forgot about the stone. Who will roll away that great stone from the entrance to the tomb?" And then they looked up and saw the place, and the stone had been rolled back already! Moreover, the tomb, when they got there, was empty. The body was gone! Trembling and fearful, for they were utterly mystified, they fled from the tomb and came to Peter and the other disciples. "Peter, Peter, they have taken away the body of our Master and we don't know where they have laid it. O Peter, what are we to do?" Then Peter and another of the disciples risked all by running in broad daylight to the garden to see for themselves. Peter was outrun and the other came first to the tomb. He peered in and saw the linen shroud lying, but he stayed outside. Then Peter arrived and jumped in. He too saw the linen shroud lying. Here was the place where the head had rested, a napkin rolled up separately and lying apart; there was the shroud laid aside; and the tomb was quite empty! The other disciple now entered and saw what Peter saw. "The head, Peter—that's where the head was; and this is how the body lay; but it's gone!" "What does it mean?" asked the awed Peter. "It means but one thing: resurrection! God has raised him from the dead. He is not here, he is risen! He has overcome death and is alive forevermore. Of course that is it. Didn't he tell us that his blood was to be poured out so that God might make a new covenant of love with his people? And God has accepted the sacrifice of his life for our sake. Dear God, that we should have walked so closely with the Son of Man and not have seen his glory!"

Jesus appeared in his risen glory to Peter, then to all the eleven disciples, and he brought to them the benediction of his peace and the power of his presence. He would nevermore be absent from them, for he lived forever in the majesty of his Father. It was the real beginning of the new age, the coming of the Kingdom of God with power. "One day," they said to one another, "our Jesus will indeed reign as King in the lives of all people; he will come again and show himself as he truly is." In their hearts they treasured up all the words he had spoken to them, and the memory of the marvelous works he had done on earth. "You must be my witnesses," he had said. "On you will fall the mantle of my Spirit and you will go preaching the great good news of God. For the new covenant is for everyone, that all may know God, from the least to the greatest. It is for the forgiveness of sins, that they may become a new people, God's people, over whom he reigns in love, until he brings all things to his appointed end. Go therefore and teach them in my name."

PART
II

The Power of the Kingdom

11 THE BAZAARS of Jerusalem were well stocked with grapes, olives, and figs, barley and wheat, and other produce brought in by the countryfolk of Judea. The whole city was looking forward with joy to the Feast of Weeks at Pentecost, the fiftieth day following the Passover; for then they celebrated harvesttide and gave thanks to the Lord for all his goodness. In the Temple the priests would sacrifice lambs and offer before God two loaves made from the new season's grain. God the Lord gave them their daily bread.

Pentecost was welcomed too by widows and orphans, by slaves and strangers in the land, for the divine law made careful provision for their welfare as dependents within the holy community. God the Lord had made all Israel a brotherhood.

So it was appropriate at this time that the Jewish nation should recall how on Mt. Sinai, long ago and soon after the very first Passover when their ancestors escaped to freedom out of Egypt, God had given to Moses the two tables of the law. These were the proof of his covenant with the children of Abraham, Isaac, and Jacob: "that he would be their God and they would be his people." From these Commandments Israel learned how to worship and how to order their social life; and in them they had the assurance that God the Lord ruled over them in justice, holiness, and love.

This year, as always, the citizens of Jerusalem waited for Pentecost, and it seemed to most of them that the life of the city was going on in a quite normal way.

But there was one group of Jews there who knew that everything had been changed this year and that life could never be the same again. Many of them still worshiped in the Temple and attended regularly the Sabbath meetings in the synagogues, yet their whole religious outlook had been altered. These people had seen the Messiah of the nation put to death at Passover; they had also seen the glory of his resurrection from the dead. Levi, Thomas, Philip of Bethsaida, and the women who had come up with Jesus and his disciples from Capernaum shared the praises and the sermons of the Galilean synagogues in Jerusalem; the rich landowner Barnabas, the cousin of John Mark, worshiped with his fellow Jews from the island of Cyprus; Lucius went with friends from Cyrene in North Africa—it was all the regular pattern of their religion hitherto when they happened to be visiting in the Holy City. Nevertheless they found themselves this year as men and women in a strange new world. They were somewhat bewildered, uncertain of the future, waiting, as some of them put it, for the skies to open and the Messiah to appear on the clouds of heaven in the divine glory of his Kingdom. Momentous things had been happening, and by the favor of God they had been privileged to take part in them.

These disciples knew that God's Kingdom had indeed come near in the amazing love, the wonderful works, and the inspired words of their Master. Jesus was no pretentious criminal who could be dismissed with priestly scorn and left to die by the roadside, like the poor fellow in his parable of the Good Samaritan. He was a reality to be reckoned with, for by the will of God and out of his own compassion and humility he had sacrificed his life for the sake of wicked men. His cross had given to the disciples immeasurable hope, because in dying Jesus had shown his incomparable greatness; and in overcoming death he had opened to them the gates of new life. Oh, it was blessed in those days to be alive, for God through his Servant had renewed the face of the earth in the most unexpected way! Soon the harvest would be reaped; soon the full glory of the Kingdom would show itself and all the kingdoms of this earth would become the Kingdom of their God and of his Christ. Pentecost without the resurrection was but a pale promise of what might yet be; but Pentecost in the certainty that Jesus lived would be of all the days the happiest and the best.

As yet, however, the men and women who shared the faith that Jesus had risen were disorganized and not quite sure of themselves. They could not tell how strict a watch might be kept on the followers of Jesus by the authorities. They wondered if it would be safe for the leading disciples to show themselves openly in the courtyards of the Temple. They debated whether they were to go out, as once before, two by two, preaching the good news of the Kingdom. The Master might be alive and exalted, but they needed his leadership there and then.

No doubt the Roman procurator and his advisers would dismiss the idea that provincial followers of a dead and discredited rebel could provoke further mischief and endanger security. But Annas, Caiaphas, and the other members of the Jewish Sanhedrin were not at ease. Some of them realized that in Jesus of Nazareth they had had to deal with a most unusual claimant to the rank and title of King-Messiah. These Jewish leaders would therefore be on guard against any hotheaded disciples who might try in their Master's name to seek vengeance and to overthrow his enemies. The peace of the State and the safety of religion would have to be insured, and the high priest with all his family protected. Rome would provide them with all the crosses they required to crush any new rebellion that used the name of Jesus!

All this and more was known to Peter, James, and John, the three who had stood closest to Jesus, and so they stayed often indoors and shut themselves up for fear of the Jews. During the weeks before the harvest thanksgiving they spent many an evening with other sympathizers in that upper room of the house where John Mark lived with his mother. This room was a holy place for all of them, full of the dearest memories, fragrant with the presence and the benediction of their Lord. Here he had taken their daily bread and made it an effective symbol and sign of himself, broken in death that they might learn to love God and love one another. Here he had pledged them in a cup of love a new and precious covenant that God the Father was enacting between the company of disciples and himself, because

Jesus was to shed his blood in sacrifice. It had been here that Jesus had in this way, and in his farewell messages, constituted his own followers as a new and holier brotherhood. To them he had given the benefits and the privileges of God's long-expected Kingdom. If they loved him and kept his commandments, God the Father, he had told them, would dwell in them and they in him; and by this union they would find continual fellowship with their Teacher and Lord and a new source of power. And it was in this very room that Jesus had revealed himself to his beloved in the mystery of the resurrection. He had brought them forgiveness, he had pardoned their desertion, he had made them wait for the next move in the divine campaign to conquer the world by the power of love. Behind the locked doors of this room, then, they felt secure. Closeted here with their Master, they must be defended from his foes. The reality of heaven filled their hearts as they talked together of him who had been their light, the Sun of righteousness risen with healing in his wings—the Man who had opened their eyes to see new meanings in the name of Father. As they searched the prophets and read diligently in all the Scriptures, their hearts burned within them, and they began to understand more deeply and more truly how the Messiah of the Lord could be the Servant of God who gave his life a ransom for others.

It was not always easy. Despite the magnificence of their resurrection faith there were dark and trying days when they did not see the way ahead. If they reminded one another that Jesus had defined discipleship as taking up a cross and following him, they had now to discover precisely what this might mean, since Jesus had taken up the cross alone. How could they share the ministry and the destiny of the Son of Man when they no longer enjoyed his constant presence and could not hear him speak in the old familiar

way? For the risen Christ did not eat with them and sleep
with them, as in Galilee, in the regions about Tyre and
Sidon, at Caesarea Philippi, and in Jerusalem. They did
have high moments of prayer, communion—and vision—
when they became assured of his triumph and continued
life. He might be as close to them as God was; yet, like God,
he was not right there in person in the room with them as
once he had been in the days of his flesh. For Jesus was Lord,
exalted to the "right hand of God" in heaven.

Thus they waited, encouraged by the vocation Jesus had
brought to them, to be his witnesses, and sustained by the
promise he had left with them, that they would receive
power. But they could not help being aware of the con-
tradictions in their experience. Peter in particular, the rock
among the believers, found that his life was made up of
hope and fear, joy and despair, uncertainty and wonder,
and sometimes sheer panic.

Pentecost came at last and they were all assembled in
their usual meeting place. When they began to celebrate
the thanksgiving, it became suddenly a rapture and a miracle. It was early in the morning and they were recounting
all those blessings for which they had to be grateful, over
and above the ordinary joy in the early summer harvest of
the fields. Jesus their Lord was not dead but alive! By word
and miracle he had declared to them the charm and power
of the Kingdom. He had assured them that, where a few
were gathered in the power of his name and under his
direction, he himself would be there in their midst.

Suddenly, as they talked and sang, helping one another
to praise their fathers' God, one here and another there
discovered how real was that promise of the Master. He
was in the midst of them, in the laughter and the prayer,
in the songs and the memories, in the adoration and the
hope that filled them all. As the risen Lord, he was being

revealed to them in a new manner; they were seeing themselves afresh as the company of men and women who were bound together by the supernatural love of God; whom Jesus had not been ashamed to call his brethren; who were living branches in the Vine of God. The inspiration of his love and the deathless glory of his person opened their hearts and minds to unfathomable joy and the inbreathing of spiritual power. It was marvelous and supernatural to them. This experience together of the radiant splendor of the risen Jesus, this profound sense of their unity in him, brought to each one of them a sensation of overwhelming divine power and wisdom entering into them.

Some told afterward how a mighty, rushing wind had blown through the house and shaken them all; and indeed the Spirit of God who is the Wind of heaven had breathed into them new qualities of soul and stirred up in them new energies of mind and will. Others told how they had seemed to see a strange, unearthly fire spitting out tongues of flame; and indeed this was how in days of old the divine Spirit had appeared to illumine some of the prophets. They all agreed that in the ecstasy of their vision they felt themselves bound in body and spirit to Jesus their Lord and to each other.

The expression of their wonder and joy took different forms. There was singing; there was praying; there was much excitement. To Peter the visitation brought an assurance he had lacked, and a quieting of his fears. He felt called again to offer that leadership to which Jesus had appointed him at Caesarea Philippi, to be the man of faith upon whom others might lean.

Excited, elated, expectant, the disciples of Jesus ran out among the people of Jerusalem and their actions caused amazement. Their words and their songs sounded to many of the passers-by like gibberish; others thought they could make out words in strange languages. "Look at them," people cried, "these men are intoxicated. They must have been drinking new wine!" But Peter, confident and fearless, stood up in defense of the disciples.

"Men of Judea and residents in Jerusalem! These men are not drunk, as you imagine. It is only nine in the morning and no one in his senses consumes quantities of wine so early in the day.

"I shall tell you what this means. God has fulfilled the ancient prophecy of Joel that reads:

" 'And it shall come to pass in the last days, says the Lord,
That I shall pour out my spirit upon all men.
Your sons and your daughters will prophesy,
Your young men will see visions,
And your old men will dream dreams.
Yes, on my servants, both men and women,
Shall I then pour out my spirit, and they will be prophets.'

"Listen to me, you men of Israel, the people of God. Jesus of Nazareth preached in this city not many weeks ago, bringing to you the good news of God's Kingdom which would mean the end of this age. As many of you know well, God approved him to us by signs and wonders; but you and your rulers rejected him. Even so, it was in the divine purpose for our salvation that you arrested Jesus and had him crucified by the Romans at Passover. We who are his disciples are here to witness to you this day that Jesus is not dead! For death could not hold him, the Holy One of God. He is the true Messiah of our nation and God has vindicated him by raising him from the dead to the place of royal dignity and glory at his right hand. He has been revealed to us in his risen life; and now this has happened.

"Men and brethren, it is a marvelous thing that has been done this day. For you can see for yourselves how the disciples of Jesus have received the divine gift and have become prophets. Exalted with God, Jesus has poured out the long-promised power of the Spirit and brought to us all the beginning of the new age. Jesus reigns in heaven and God is establishing his Kingdom among you!"

This preaching struck home to many in the crowd who knew about Jesus and his crucifixion. Above the cross men had read the words of accusation, "Jesus of Nazareth, the King of the Jews," and here were men and women who claimed that miracles had taken place and that Jesus was in truth their King. Their Messiah! The One who should deliver them out of the hands of their enemies! Oh, what glories there might yet be in Israel!

"Brethren," they cried out, "what are we to do? How can we share in the Kingdom of your Jesus?"

"Save yourselves from this wicked generation," answered Peter. "Repent of your evil life and turn again to God. Believe with us that Jesus is the Servant of the Lord and the rightful Messiah of Israel. Then come and be baptized with water for the removal of your sins and you too will receive this gift of the Spirit. For the divine promise is intended for you and for your children, and it is for all of Israel who are far away!"

To these urgings and entreaties hundreds responded and came forward for baptism. Soon many groups of believers were meeting in the homes of leading disciples to learn more about the ministry and message of Jesus. In obedience to his purpose they broke bread after his example at the Last Supper, and as they did so they were knit together in one mind and one heart. Happiness and joy filled every day, for the love that had been seen in Jesus became more and more the distinctive mark of the society. Courage and power had replaced earlier doubts and fears, so that they preached openly the good news of God.

Before long, however, they learned the truth of their

Master's prediction that his disciples must share the lot of the Son of Man by suffering and tribulation in the world.

One afternoon Peter and John were going into the Temple to pray when a lame beggar asked them for charity. The two disciples looked at him intently, and then Peter said, "Look at us." The beggar paid attention to them, expecting to receive something. But Peter went on: "Silver and gold I do not possess; but what I have I give to you. In the name of Jesus the Messiah, the Nazarene, walk!" Gripping him by the right hand, Peter lifted him up, and at once his feet and ankles gained strength; he jumped up and stood on his legs, then he began to walk and followed the disciples into the Temple court, leaping for joy and praising God. Those who saw this were awe-struck.

When a crowd had gathered round the three men, Peter explained that it was no merit or magic in John or himself that had effected the cure. It was faith in Jesus the Messiah and the exercise of divine power through the invocation of the holy name. Once again he called his listeners to penitence and faith, as he told them about Jesus and the resurrection.

The priests and the Sadducees acted instantly to stop this dangerous preaching and ordered the captain of the Temple police to arrest Peter and John. Before the Sanhedrin, Peter boldly told his story and both men impressed the council with their bearing. Here were no "illiterate fisherfolk," as some had contemptuously said, but men who had been with Jesus and were determined to continue his mission. After a private conference, the Sanhedrin ordered Peter and John never again to teach in the name of Jesus.

"Judge for yourselves," said the prisoners, "if we ought to listen to you or to God. So far as we are concerned, we must proclaim the wonderful things we have both heard and seen. We must obey God rather than men!" Fearing a popular rising, the court was content to have them flogged and then released them with dark threats about future punishment if they should persist in this preaching. Not at all daunted, the disciples continued to defy the edict, rejoicing that they had been found worthy to suffer for Jesus' sake. Through them the Kingdom of God was still fighting its battle for right over wrong, for love over hate.

Difficulties arose even among themselves. The richer disciples, in order to fulfill the rule of brotherly love, sold their property and paid in the proceeds to a common fund, from which disbursements were made to the poor and needy. Common meals were arranged; the sick were cared for; clothing was provided and rooms rented. All this laid heavy burdens on the leaders, whose primary duty was to preach and teach. Soon complaints were laid by those who came from distant lands of the Jewish Dispersion. These people spoke the common Greek of the Roman world. The charge was that the charitable distribution of money and food was being done by Aramaic-speaking men who were not as fair to the Greek-speaking poor as to the rest. "Our widows are being neglected," the Hellenists said.

To meet this problem and relieve the leaders, the congregation appointed seven officers to take care of the common meals and the charity. All the men chosen were wise, diligent, and marked out by spiritual power. One was a Syrian from Antioch called Nicolaus; two others, Philip and Stephen, had special gifts for preaching; and the other four, like these three, were originally from beyond Palestine: Parmenas, Timon, Prochorus, and Nicanor were their names. After prayer, the leaders gave the seven authority for their ministry by laying their hands upon them in Jewish fashion.

Stephen was a man of exceptional insight, and he was not content to serve only in the administration of charity.

He was ambitious to preach Jesus and the new age of the Kingdom. Stephen believed that both the Old Testament and the teaching of Jesus implied that God the Father would rule over all the nations, and so he was eager to bring in those who were not Jews. Had not Jesus cleansed the Temple and declared that it was to be a place of prayer for all peoples? For similar reasons Stephen believed that the law of Moses could not be accepted just as it stood, and on all these points he argued powerfully with other Greek-speaking Jews in the synagogue of the Libertines. His opponents included men from Cyrene, Egypt, Asia, and Cilicia; one of the Cilicians was a certain Saul of Tarsus who was frequently called by his Roman name of Paul and was regarded as a most promising student of the law. Saul of Tarsus belonged to the strictest party of the Pharisees.

Stephen's attack on the central place of the Temple and the exclusive privileges of Jews stirred up a bitter controversy. One day a mob seized him and rushed him before the Sanhedrin. "This fellow," they charged, "has blasphemed against the Temple and the law; he is a bigoted follower of Jesus the Nazarene and we heard him say that this Jesus will destroy the Temple and alter the customs we have received from Moses."

"Are these statements true?" asked the high priest.

"Fathers and brethren," began Stephen, "you all know how God made the covenant with Abraham and later raised up Moses to deliver our nation from captivity in Egypt. Under Moses a tent for the worship of God was set up in the wilderness; nevertheless our fathers refused to worship truly and they bowed down before a calf of gold. Under Joshua the tent was brought to this land, and later still King David requested permission to build God a more fitting dwelling. It was Solomon, however, who built the first Temple, for David was not found worthy to do so. Yet

the Most High does not dwell in tents or temples, the work
of men's hands. Isaiah says: 'Heaven is my throne, and the
earth a footstool for my feet. What sort of house then will
you build for me? says the Lord; what resting place shall I
enjoy? Did not my hands form the universe?'"

Stephen got no farther with the argument to which all
this was leading; carried away by his intense emotion he
burst out:

"Stiff-necked creatures that you are! uncircumcised in
ears and heart, who can neither hear the word of God nor
serve the Holy Spirit! You are just like your fathers who
constantly fought against God and persecuted his prophets;
for now you yourselves have slain the Holy One of God.
What good is the law to people like you, who received it
through the angels but have not obeyed it? Murderers . . .
disobedient . . . traitors to the Lord . . ."

What an uproar followed! Priests and scribes tore their
clothes and ground their teeth. Then Stephen looked up.
"I see the heavens opened," he cried, "and Jesus, the Son
of Man, standing at the right hand of the glory of God!"
That was the end. In a body they rushed at Stephen and in
mob fury they hauled him outside the city limits. They had
no authority to condemn to death and carry out the penalty
without permission from the Romans, but the times were
troubled and the procurator absent. "Blasphemer," they
shouted. "Death to the blasphemer! He has attacked the
holy place and the holy law, and by our law he ought to die.
Stone him; stone the blasphemer as we are commanded in
the law!"

And there the priests pelted the young man Stephen,
helped by the enraged citizens and the fanatical scribes;
one of the Pharisees who stood by and watched it done was
Saul of Tarsus. Nothing could save the victim. Hundreds
of loose stones, some being large boulders, lay to hand in

the great pit into which they crowded him; and eager hands took aim, eager men of God grew more vehement and vicious when his nose bled and his eyes were struck. Before long a young man's life was ebbing out in agony because of that cruel sport and judgment. As he weakened in the hot sun, he called on his Lord, "Receive my spirit," and before his bloody eyes were closed in death his parched lips muttered the incredible intercession, "Lord, count not this sin against them!"

Buried beneath that heap of bitter stones, Stephen died, cursed as a blasphemer; but at once he was revered as a martyr, and the followers of Jesus, for whom he gave his life, took heart again. Pious friends came to find his poor battered body and gave it honorable burial, making loud lamentation over a lovely life in which the Spirit of the Messiah Jesus, the Son of God, had found a welcome and a home.

The outbreak by the mob led to inquisition about other followers of Jesus holding views like Stephen's, and as a result most of the congregation were scattered over the length and breadth of the land. Only devout leaders like James the Just, the brother of Jesus, could safely remain in Jerusalem, for they had no desire to make a final break with the nation of Israel, nor to spread doctrines that would disrupt the peace and lead to riot. Stephen had done this because he had seen more clearly than they the ends to which the teaching of Jesus led. Fleeing from the anger of the priests and the lawyers of Judaism, the disciples scattered to Damascus in the north, to the countryside of Samaria, to the coasts of Phoenicia, and even to islands like Cyprus. Wherever they went, they took with them the gospel of the Lord who had died and risen again.

Philip, one of the seven officers of charity, conducted a mission in Samaria with considerable success. He was here, there, and everywhere in his enthusiasm. Once on the road from Jerusalem to Gaza he fell in with the chamberlain of Queen Candace, the sovereign of the Ethiopians; this man was a convert to the Jewish religion who had been on pilgrimage to Jerusalem and was going home. Philip joined him and discovered that he was reading from the Scriptures. The passage was from the fifty-third chapter of Isaiah, which runs: "He was led like a sheep to the slaughter and, as a lamb before its shearers is dumb, so he opened not his mouth. In his humiliation justice was removed from him; and who will explain his generation? For his life has been taken from the earth." "Tell me of whom the prophet is speaking," said the chamberlain. Then Philip began to show him that this prophecy could be applied best to the ministry of Jesus, the Servant of God, who had given his life in great humility that others might be saved from their sins. Disciples of Jesus were the heirs of the Kingdom of God and their lives were transformed by the power of God's Spirit.

Soon they came to a stream of running water. "If all this is true," said the chamberlain, "and I believe it is, I should like to become a disciple. Here is water: is there anything to prevent my being baptized?" Philip gladly granted his request and baptized this Ethiopian believer into the name of Jesus. Immediately afterward he left his new friend and, under the impulse of the Spirit, hurried to Azotus and then northward along the shore to Herod's city of Caesarea. In every town and village that he passed through he preached the gospel.

The spread of Christian settlements in Palestine had been rapid and astonishing; they were to be found in Judea, Samaria, and Galilee, and now Philip had evangelized the coastland. Wherever it was accepted with trust, the gospel was creating a common attitude of devotion to God the Father and bringing into ordinary human lives the love that was the supreme fruit of the Spirit of Jesus. Men and women testified that despite their faults and weakness in moral endeavor they were learning to be gracious, to serve others, to live in hope that evil could be overcome. Of course the deep-rooted selfishness of men brought problems and sufferings, but the believers found a divine power working within them. They could face martyrdom for the sake of Jesus. Even among Samaritans and strangers like the Ethiopian the gospel was proving its vitality and its range, and the Kingdom of God was taking root. People who had eyes to see actually could observe in all this spiritual renewal the reality of the Kingdom that Jesus had preached: for the Kingdom had come with power.

Ambassadors of the Kingdom

12 THE MAN who was hurrying secretly to Jerusalem from the north was Saul the Cilician Jew, who was often called Paul. Nearly three years ago he had stood and watched the merciless priests and the infuriated mob stone to death the young Christian Stephen, and he had been glad that this enemy of God and true religion was receiving the just reward for his blasphemies.

But the Paul who traveled so carefully toward the city and the Temple was not in the least the same man spiritually as that earlier spectator of a martyrdom. For now he himself professed the faith for which Stephen had died; he was a man whose life had been turned upside down.

It was with very mixed feelings that he wondered about the welcome he might receive when he reached his journey's end, for friends of the old days would now be his enemies and former enemies might well be suspicious of him, so sudden, so strange, so utterly unexpected had been his rightabout-face. As he drew nearer he could not help thinking of far-off days when for the first time he had approached Jerusalem; of the home in Tarsus he had left; of the godly parents who had been so scrupulous in training him in the ways of his fathers. Would they disown him now as a turncoat? In the alien atmosphere of Tarsus, with its pagan ways and culture, it had never been easy to avoid the defilements of Gentiles and adhere to the purity of Judaism. But Paul had done so. Many could support his boast that from his youth he had observed the Jewish law in every detail. Even in the sight of God, the holy Lord, he believed that his life had been blameless. Hadn't he been a Pharisee of the Pharisees, an ardent student of the Scriptures, the kind of pupil about whom his teachers had predicted great things? He had been an aggressive and dogmatic debater, a man passionately convinced that his own views were right. If he stumbled now and again in his speech, if he had gained no prizes for rhetoric, he was nevertheless the kind of young man that Judaism needed. He was a rock upon whom weaker brethren could lean. Moreover, Paul had been one of those devout nationalists who let politics and armed force alone, but dreamed all the more hopefully that God would send his Messiah to liberate the Jews and establish his Kingdom.

And then he had encountered the happy followers of Jesus, the men and women whose very lives proclaimed that they had been changed profoundly by their faith. Blind that he was, he had rushed in to challenge them with mere words. They had tried to show him out of the Scriptures that a crucified carpenter from Galilee was the long-awaited Messiah and that the new age had already dawned! As if any good thing could come out of half-pagan Galilee! Their nonsense had infuriated him. He had resented their patient and gentle ways. He scoffed at their silly interpretations of Isaiah. Didn't they know that in the law it was written explicitly that a man who had hung on a tree until he died must be under God's curse? Jesus of Nazareth could not possibly be the Lord's Anointed! The whole idea was fantastic. It was true that every report agreed that this Jesus had been a humble and loving man, tender and kind to the poor, to the outcast, and to women and children. Much that he was said to have taught was penetrating and wise. But that made it all the more shocking to Paul that Jesus had been so vehement in his opposition to the traditions and practice of the Pharisees, his own teachers, accusing them of the worst kinds of hypocrisy! All the Jew in him had revolted with scorn and bitterness against the Galilean and his deluded disciples, and he had looked on coldly while the holy men and the unholy mob pelted young Stephen till he died. Not because he thought that Stephen was wicked; Stephen was simply a misguided fanatic who did not see that Judaism must be preserved entirely and that all the nations were bound in the end to submit themselves to its rule and its God. In the synagogue of the Cilicians Paul had set his idea of a universal dominion for the national religion over against Stephen's; he had told the passionate Christian to his face that the spread of his views would shake Judaism to its foundations: and that was why Stephen had had to die.

Yet now the former persecutor, who had left with formal authority from the highest priestly leaders to hunt out and persecute the followers of Jesus, was stealing back into Jerusalem incognito, a convert to Stephen's faith and the slave of Stephen's Lord! He was running for his life from Damascus where enemies had lain in ambush to arrest or murder him; and soon, very soon now, he must find the fisherman Simon, the leader of the Christians in the city, the one they called in Aramaic *"Cephas"* and in Greek *"Petros,"* because Jesus had designated him as the "Rock" among his disciples. He must find Peter and see how the land lay.

Once inside Jerusalem Paul sought out a wealthy man from Cyprus, called Barnabas. At least Barnabas had been rich, but he had sold his property on the island of Cyprus and contributed the proceeds to the funds of the Christian community. Paul had been acquainted with him in earlier days and hoped that he would befriend him.

Barnabas was well named "the son of consolation," and to Paul's relief he lived up to his name, receiving Paul with kind hospitality and accepting him without reserve as a brother in Christ. The next day Barnabas and the new arrival made their way cautiously to the home of John Mark, the cousin of Barnabas, where they were certain to meet the leading disciples.

"Simon Peter, I want you to know Paul of Tarsus, who has just arrived from Damascus and is one of us now. Paul, I want you to know James, the brother of our Lord Jesus, to whom the Lord appeared after his resurrection. Peter and James, as I told you, are the leaders of our brotherhood in Jerusalem."

The former fisherman, the former carpenter, and the former student had come face to face at last some three years after Paul's conversion, and thus momentous associations began. The believers in Jerusalem had known about

the conversion, of course, but their information was scanty
and rather inaccurate. Paul now spent two weeks with these
leaders and gave them his fullest confidence. First they had
to hear the dramatic story of the great turning point in his
career.

Doubtless in such words as he used often later in his life
he told them how he had been brought up in Tarsus, a
college city in the province of Cilicia and of no mean reputation: he had been circumcised, as the law of Moses required, on the eighth day of life; his family was genuinely
of Israel, the chosen people of God, belonging to the tribe
of Benjamin. His parents were faithful Jews living among
Gentiles, but they had not forgotten the language of their
fathers. In young manhood he had become an adherent of
the Pharisees, and he had tried with all his heart and mind
to observe every detail of the law and all the traditions of his
teachers. Then, as they well knew, he had met Stephen and
the Christians and had bound himself to eliminate their
heresy from Judaism.

"I set out from Jerusalem to travel to Damascus, and I
carried papers from the high priests requiring the local
synagogue authorities there to arrest and punish any followers of the Nazarenes in Syria. Some distance south of
Damascus I was stopped suddenly in my tracks by the
strangest experience of my life. On the very road of my
hostility God had pursued and overtaken me, and there
it pleased him to reveal his Son in my own life. In a flash
I was struck blind by a supernatural brightness that shone
all about me, and I fell to the ground. I was aware of One
who showed himself to me in the center of the light. 'Sir,'
I faltered, 'who are you?' 'I am Jesus,' he said, 'whom you
are persecuting by attacking my friends. It is hard for you
to kick against the goad. Rise, Saul of Tarsus, and be my
servant, for I have chosen you to declare my glory in the

Gentile world.' I was completely shaken by the vision and let myself be led into Damascus, where Christian brethren cared for me. Ananias gave me instruction in the faith and I acknowledged that Jesus is Lord; then my sight and strength were restored; I received baptism into the name of Jesus and was welcomed by the brotherhood in Damascus as a fellow believer.

"Now that Jesus has become my Master, I have to confess that all my life hitherto was fruitless and ungodly, and I have to ask pardon of every disciple for my folly and my enmity. I know now that love is the fulfillment of the law, and that a man may keep the letter but neglect the spirit of the law. That is just what I did. I have been cruel and harsh to those who did not see my point of view; I have been the prisoner of envy, for in my heart I was covetous. Oh, the anguish of it—to will what is right but not to do it! The good that I wanted to do, I failed to do, and the evil that I did not want to do was the very thing I did. But thanks be to God, he is giving me victory through our Lord Jesus!

"Soon after my conversion I went off into desert solitudes in the kingdom of Aretas, to consider what God required of me in my new life. I had troubles there that I need not describe, and came back to Damascus. There I entered the synagogues in fear and trembling, to preach to the Jews the faith I once had attacked. That made me more enemies! Agents of King Aretas, acting on information from the local Jews, tried to arrest me; but just as his police were going to pounce, our friends got wind of it. They rushed me by the back lanes to the city wall and let me down in a basket of rushes, and so I escaped and fled in disguise to Jerusalem. That is how I come to be here."

Peter and James in turn told Paul much that he did not know as yet about the life and teaching of the Lord. Peter had seen the marvelous works of the Kingdom and knew of the long nights Jesus had spent in the hills alone in prayer. He told Paul many parables of the Kingdom, delighting to instruct in the Way of Jesus this learned young man whom God had called to serve. His eyes shone as he told Paul and lived over again the days and nights he had shared with Jesus in Galilee and Judea. He pictured Jesus on that last journey to Jerusalem, his face set like a flint in his resolve to do and dare everything for the Kingdom of his Father. With sad pride he described the Last Supper and the scene in the Garden, the arrest and the crucifixion, for in the telling he had to recall his own denials and shame. And then he went on to tell Paul how Jesus had risen and appeared to him, later to the eleven disciples, and to James, and to the great company on the Day of Pentecost.

Fortified by all this interchange of remembrance and by the friendship of his brother Christians, Paul went out boldly to preach in the synagogues of Jerusalem. But this rash zeal was simply asking for trouble and perhaps for stoning, a calamity that the brotherhood could not permit. Paul was sent off secretly to Caesarea where Philip was at work; and from Caesarea he took ship for Cilicia and home.

Peter had the responsibility of caring for new centers of faith among the Jews as a result of the evangelism. With John the son of Zebedee he visited Samaria and confirmed them in the way of discipleship; later he went to the Mediterranean coast, traveling by Emmaus to Lydda and Joppa. For some time he stayed in Joppa at the house of another Simon, a trader in leather.

One day messengers arrived from Caesarea, the provincial capital, with a request from a captain in the Roman garrison called Cornelius. They came to the door of Simon's house and inquired if a man called Simon Peter was staying there. Peter was informed and introduced himself as the one they were seeking. When they told him that a Gentile soldier wanted him to come to Caesarea for a conference about this gospel of the Kingdom that Philip and others like him were preaching, Peter was surprised and at first hesitant about going. It was unlawful for a Jew to enter a Gentile home or to eat with Gentiles, for they did not keep the dietary rules of the law. Contact with Gentiles made a good Jew religiously "unclean." Peter as a disciple of Jesus was still a good Jew and he wondered how his loyalty to the law might be affected by any such conference regarding the gospel. The local Christians of Joppa were anxious also, but in the end they decided to go.

Peter's mind was made up as he thought about the meaning of a strange vision that had come to him on the roof of Simon's house just before the messengers from Cornelius were announced. He had been hungry when he went up at noon to pray. He seemed to fall into a trance and saw a great sheet let down from the sky. All kinds of food were in it, including pigs, cattle, and birds. "Rise, Peter, and eat," said a voice. "No, Lord," answered Peter, "it has never been my custom to eat what is unclean. I observe the law." Then the voice spoke again, telling him that he must not think unclean what God himself had cleansed. At that moment a servant had come to tell him that strangers from Caesarea were looking for him.

With some members of the Joppa congregation Peter set off, and after two days on the road they arrived in Caesarea. Cornelius had gathered a group of his relatives and intimates to meet Peter, and when the missionary arrived, the Roman captain prostrated himself before him. "Stand up, please," said the embarrassed Peter, "for I am just a man like yourself." Then he entered the house, explaining to his host why he, a Jew, was willing to visit in a Gentile home.

"It is my conviction that your God intended me to meet you," said Cornelius, after he had heard about Peter's vision and its message. "I too had a vision and I was commanded to send for you."

Peter was astonished. "I see that God does not make the distinctions between people that we do," he said, and thereupon began to preach.

"As you may have heard, God sent his word to the Jews in the person of Jesus of Nazareth, whom we call Lord. After John the Baptist had prepared the way, Jesus came into Galilee, teaching that the Kingdom of God was at the door and that men should repent and believe the good news. He drove out evil spirits in the power of God's Spirit and cured many of their diseases. He fed a multitude in the desert, brought new life to the dying, and even calmed the waters for us in the storms of the Lake of Galilee. But the leaders of our nation would not believe that Jesus was the Messiah; they convicted him falsely of blasphemy and denounced him to the Romans for high treason. They scourged him, mocked him, and led him away to death; yet he offered them no provocation. When he was reviled, he reviled not again. He was led like a lamb to the slaughter and gave his life for love of his people. Like all the others, I deserted him; but, to my shame, I also denied him with oaths and curses. When he was put to death on the cross, we thought that the light had gone out forever and that God had deserted us.

"Then, two days after the crucifixion, early in the morning of the first day of the week, some women of our company who had gone to the tomb to anoint his body came running in terror to us. They said they had seen an angel who told them, 'He is not here; he has risen from the dead and gone ahead to Galilee, just as he told the disciples.' It was perfectly true, for we have seen him alive, and now we preach in his name the glad news of God's Kingdom. The love of Jesus has taken possession of us and made us new men and women; our sins have been forgiven; we are learning to be humble, single-minded, people who put first the glory of God our Father and who renounce wealth and power in this world. Those who accept our message and repent also receive fresh gifts of spiritual power. We believe that a new age . . ."

Peter stopped speaking. An air of tension had become noticeable in the room, as Cornelius and his friends paid eager attention to the gospel. These were no ordinary pagans, but eager seekers after truth who were dissatisfied with the cults and philosophies of the Roman world. What they had heard of the work of Philip had made them anxious to know more from the leader of the Christians; they were already "not far from the Kingdom" and now the words of Peter had warmed their hearts and moved them to contrition for wasted lives and false ideals. Prompted by their need and their longing, they assented with heart and voice to the preaching. Jesus seemed to lay his spell upon them and they cried out, "Jesus *Kyrios,* Jesus is Lord"; they began to pray and to sing; and Peter could not proceed. The brethren from Joppa were equally amazed at this unheard-of thing: here were Gentiles, aliens from the commonwealth of Israel, with no claim to the covenant promises God had made to Abraham and Moses; and yet these foreigners had received the same tokens of the divine Spirit that had been given so wonderfully on the Day of Pentecost in the upper room to the first congregation in Jerusalem. "Glory be to God!" they cried in joyful excitement; and Peter turned to them to say, "Surely they belong with us and no one can hinder their baptism!"

In this way Cornelius and his household joined the rapidly growing Christian movement; another Pentecost of the Spirit had been celebrated in an alien place and the power of the Kingdom had reached out to transform the lives even of Gentiles. Stephen had been right!

But when Peter returned to Jerusalem, there were some Jewish Christians who objected to what had been done. In their judgment the proper thing in the case of Gentiles like Cornelius would have been to make them Jews first. This could be done by circumcising and baptizing the men, and by baptizing the women. Only then could they qualify for membership in God's Kingdom by faith in Jesus as the Messiah. This procedure had been followed with Nicolaus of Antioch and the chamberlain of Queen Candace; to accept non-Jews without first making them Jews raised a whole new issue, and they were alarmed by its implications. This issue was destined to threaten the very existence of the Christian fellowship and to split the community in two.

Other difficulties beset them in Jerusalem. The original sharing of wealth had spent itself and many were desperately poor. Jesus had not returned, and there was no indication that the coming of the Kingdom would mean honor and riches for the disciples. Some were disappointed, for they still could not understand. The civil government also caused them anxiety. Herod Agrippa I, the successor of Herod Antipas in Galilee and Perea, had become by the favor of the Romans the ruler of Samaria and Judea. He knew well the rebellious element among the Jews, and he had received information about the Nazarene and his sect. Herod was resolved to have trouble from neither Jew nor Nazarene, and in a swift move his police arrested Peter and put James the son of Zebedee to death.

Peter miraculously escaped from prison and late one night came to the house of John Mark's mother. "Go and see who is there, Rhoda," the mistress said to the maid-servant, and the family held their breath. The girl ran back screaming, "It is Peter the apostle—or his ghost—out in the courtyard!" "You must be mad, Rhoda; something has frightened the wits out of you!" they told her. "Peter is locked up in Herod's jail." But Rhoda was right. Like a man rescued from the dead, Peter had come to leave a message for James the Just, the brother of Jesus, who would have to take charge of the Christian congregation in the Holy City. As mysteriously as he had come, Peter slipped off into the safety of the night and further adventures for the Kingdom of God and his Christ.

Mission and Crisis

13 FROM ROME, Cyrene, and Greece; from Egypt, Asia, and Palestine, visitors and traders, soldiers and preachers came to the port of Seleucia and went up the River Orontes to mingle in Syrian Antioch, the beautiful "Queen of the East." Once Antioch had been the imperial capital of Seleucid kings, successors in Persia and Asia to the incomparable Macedonian, Alexander the Great. Now it was the home of Greeks and Macedonians, the children of Alexander's armies. They shared with Syrians and Jews the political order of the Romans, the learning of the Greeks, and the voluptuous delights of Orientals.

A famous aqueduct carried water from Daphne to Antioch some four or five hundred feet below and five miles distant. Gleaming in the sun high above the river valley, its majestic citadel, the Acropolis, stood guard on Mt. Stauris. Below, on an island in the Orontes, was another walled quarter where men and women worked and played; more streets of lovely villas crept up neighboring Mt. Silpius. But the glory of the city and the hub of its life lay in the plain. Here was the forum for trade and conversation, as well as temples, baths, and other public buildings. Here were two magnificent highways, one of them memorable for the colonnades erected in Antioch's honor by Herod the Great, who had ruled in Galilee and Judea. On holidays the crowds flocked to see the games in the circus, and there was never any lack of opportunity for pleasure and excitement.

Antioch was a city of lust and vice as well as commerce. If all that men whispered was even half true, not all the water that flowed in a man's lifetime through the aqueduct from Daphne would have sufficed to purify its homes and gardens. The cypress groves of Daphne too were notorious for open immoralities, none the better for being done at the shrine of the goddess Athena. Amid Eastern splendor the Antiochenes diced, wined, and prostituted themselves, and from their city the influence of its squalid immodesty radiated into the rest of the Empire till even the Orontes became a synonym for all that was unclean and licentious.

Nevertheless, the place was highly religious in its own fashion; for the Antiochenes invoked a multitude of gods from Macedonia and Greece, as well as Astarte, the Syrian goddess of love, and the Great Mother Cybele, and even divine heroes like the Seleucid kings and the Roman emperors. For the payment of suitable fees and by secret initiation ceremonies some cults promised good health, good luck, and immortal life hereafter. People frightened by the fates; people who had known sudden misfortune and bereavement; those who were anxious to have assurance that life was meaningful, all tried to find help and satisfaction in the secret brotherhoods of these cults. Antioch was easygoing and tolerant about religious practice, so that it was no surprise that it allowed unusual freedom to the many Jews in its midst. They were granted civil rights and worshiped every Sabbath, near the river, in their own synagogues.

After the martyrdom of Stephen in Jerusalem, some Christian refugees fled northward to Damascus and beyond, finally finding safety among the industrious Jews of Syrian Antioch. They were mostly people of Cyprus and Cyrene. In the beautiful city that was now to be their home they began at once to tell others about the Kingdom of God and invited them to share their fellowship. They were so successful that soon the believers were distinctive enough and well enough known to be given first of all in Antioch the nickname "Christians."

When the congregation in Jerusalem heard what had happened, it decided to send one of its number to guide Antioch, and chose for this purpose Barnabas the Cypriot who had befriended Paul of Tarsus. Barnabas found the believers firm in the gospel and hopeful that the leaven of the Kingdom would transform the life of the city. Many of the Christians in Antioch had come originally from the larger world of the Empire and their vision was not confined to a single province. Jews and converts to Judaism were often sympathetic to the good news, but there were others too. The Syrians, Greeks, Italians, and strangers from distant areas who put in at Seleucia and made their way to the bazaars and clubs of Antioch had to be considered. Among them were those who buried themselves in sensuous pleasures only because they had failed to find a better way of life. They might well be responsive to a message that told of the conquest of death, that offered victory over evil habits, that provided loving friends who would be loyal through good days and bad. To meet the promising situation Barnabas proposed to bring in other help.

He knew of another disciple whose mind was superlatively endowed for work in the mixed community of Antioch—Paul of Tarsus, the brilliant Jew who was convinced that God had called him to preach the gospel in Gentile lands. Paul was the man to assist Barnabas! Before long the two men met in Cilicia and Barnabas related to his friend the story of the church in Antioch: how quickly it had grown under the leadership of Symeon; Manaen, a relative of the royal Herods; Lucius of Cyrene, and himself. He told Paul that among those who had fled from Jerusalem after the murder of James the son of Zebedee was his own kinsman John Mark. There was opportunity in Antioch and it needed Paul: would Paul come and help them?

In this exciting news the man from Tarsus heard a divine call and he agreed to go at once with his old friend. The Christians of the city were equally delighted and gave him a warm welcome to their society.

By Jewish custom teachers of the law were able to earn their living in various occupations, and Paul followed the rule in his own vocation as a Christian missionary and teacher. The province of Cilicia was noted for stout goatskin fabrics that made excellent tents and Paul was a craftsman in their use. In Antioch he soon found work at his trade and was no burden on the church.

As a teacher and preacher he had much to do. Converts had to receive instruction in the faith, and with them the young men and women who were growing up in Christian families. They learned the words of Jesus and heard over and over again the story of his life, his Passion, and his triumph. On the first day of the week all the Christians of the city met together for the "Love Feast," where they broke bread; then in sharing the memorial supper of their Lord, with bread and wine, they were joined in one heart and soul to one another and to the risen Savior.

Paul found scope for all his talents in the service of the Antiochenes and taught them what he had come to know in the years since his conversion. Christians everywhere were a single people, redeemed by the death of Jesus and called to proclaim the new age of the Kingdom. The Jews had rejected the Messiah and the vocation to declare the unsearchable riches of God's grace to the world. Christians, Jews and Gentiles, carried on the work that God had given to his people.

Through this teaching the believers in Antioch learned to call their society by a familiar Greek word, ecclesia, which means "assembly." This word was used frequently in the Greek translation of the Old Testament, known to most of them; and there it denoted assemblies of Israel, God's holy nation. Now it was to become the title of the Messiah's people. They were "The Ecclesia of God"; they were "The Body of the Messiah"; and they preached the speedy victory of the Kingdom of God because the power of God's Holy Spirit had descended upon them. "Ecclesia" in English is translated "Church."

About a year after Paul had come to Antioch the leaders of the church met in solemn council to discuss measures of far-reaching importance. For Barnabas and Paul now wanted to go farther afield. Barnabas had his eye on the island of Cyprus, his family home; Paul had set his heart on preaching in the provinces of Asia Minor. The whole Roman Empire must be won for the Kingdom of God and his Christ! Paul would offer the good news to Gentiles as well as Jews and was prepared to admit them simply on the profession of their faith in Jesus. Thus he would not insist on circumcision for men and boys. This would seem to Christians of Jewish background a radical change from their faith and custom, and Paul desired the support of the whole church in Antioch for this new adventure.

He and Barnabas met, therefore, with Lucius, Manaen, Symeon, and other leaders; and they devoted themselves to prayer in order to learn the will of God. Suddenly they knew with certainty. It was as if the Spirit of God had said distinctly, "Set apart Barnabas and Paul for the work to which I have appointed them." With joyful excitement the church approved, and in the usual Jewish manner the hands of its elders, the teachers and rulers elected to rule the congregation, were laid on the chief missionaries with fervent prayer for divine favor and blessing.

John Mark was chosen to accompany Barnabas and Paul, and together they traveled down the valley of the Orontes to Seleucia. From that port they sailed to Salamis in Cyprus and proceeded through the island to Paphos. Wherever they found people willing to listen, they announced that they were heralds of the Kingdom of God; they related the story of which they never tired, the story of Jesus by whose sufferings and risen power men might be saved from evil habits and unclean desires to enter at once into the new and happy life of God's family and Church.

Next they sailed to Perga in Pamphylia, a district in Asia Minor, and at this point John Mark turned back. His heart was not in the business of taking Jesus and the Kingdom to Gentiles, and he hurried home to the security of Jerusalem.

None but the audacious could win that Roman world for Christ, and Mark had not reached the full stature of his Christian manhood. One day he would. Before many days were past he would stand, one day, by two of the foremost missionaries of the cross in the hour of their darkest trial; and then he would preserve in a new kind of book, for the persecuted church of Rome and for all generations, the gospel that Peter and Paul and his kinsman Barnabas had preached. Now he had left them, and these two, Barnabas the Cypriot and Paul the Cilician, went forward together for God's sake and in the wisdom of his Spirit.

After a tiring journey through the upland country, they entered Pisidia and reached another Antioch. This place was a Roman colony on the frontiers of Phrygia, a "little Rome" set in an alien land to be an agency for Roman civilization. As one who himself possessed from birth the high honor of Roman citizenship, Paul understood fully the pride of Antioch in its civic privileges. With his companion he stood in the spacious squares that were named for the emperors Augustus and Tiberius and saw that the people worshiped an idol called *Men*, whose sign was the head of a bull. Strength and fertility lived in the animal, but the missionaries had come with the power of God's Spirit and his immortal life of love. Paul resolved that by the grace of God the population of this Antioch would learn to exchange the symbol of the bull's head for the sign of the cross.

There were communities of Jews throughout these provinces of Asia. Accordingly, on the Sabbath, Paul and Barnabas intended to visit the local synagogue, where they would find men and women of the Jewish faith, who had heard the prophecies and who waited for the Christ. The gospel was for them first. "They are Israelites," Paul used to say, "and to them belong the covenants and the delivery of the law; the promises were made to their fathers long ago; and the

Christ himself, according to his birth, was one of them.''
Moreover, the synagogue was a strategic starting point because it attracted high-minded Gentiles to its worship.

On two Sabbaths the apostles preached in the synagogue
of Pisidian Antioch and many were interested; but some of
the Jews argued with Paul and contradicted his message.
They would not accept the crucified Jesus as Messiah and
they strongly disliked any suggestion that foreigners might
be welcomed into the divine Kingdom on easy terms. Barnabas and Paul, with their converts and sympathizers, had
to abandon the synagogue. "Very well," they said to the
Jews, "we turn to the Gentiles and we remind you of the
word of God in the prophet Isaiah, 'I have given you as a
light to the Gentiles, that you may be a savior to the ends of
the earth.' We believe that the servant of whom Isaiah
speaks is Jesus of Nazareth, for God has shown to us that the
true King-Messiah is the Servant of the Lord who gave his
life as a ransom for many.''

Believers were baptized into the name of Jesus and they
were certain that their sinful life had been pardoned; moral
power came into their hearts and they faced the future with
fresh hope. The missionaries handed on to them the tradition of the gospel and instructed them briefly in the
Christian way of life; then they appointed one or two elders
to rule them, and commended them to God. They themselves had to move on.

From Pisidian Antioch they had a choice of routes: they
could travel north by Ancyra toward Bithynia; to the west,
the much used valley of the Cayster beckoned them to Ephesus, the chief city of the province of Asia; to the east lay
southern Galatia with the towns of Iconium, Lystra, and
Derbe. After prayerful consideration they turned to the
east.

In the towns of Galatia the same pattern of preaching,

strong Jewish opposition and some Gentile conversions, repeated itself. At Lystra they were attacked and Paul barely escaped with his life. What happened was that Paul commanded a lame man to stand and walk, and he did so, to the amazement of the people. They thought that the gods Zeus and Hermes had come down to visit them, and their priests prepared to garland the missionaries with flowers and sacrifice choice young bullocks in their honor. Paul managed to explain to them that he and Barnabas were but men, preachers of a new gospel. He was interrupted by the arrival of Jews from Iconium who roused the crowd against the preachers. Barnabas got away, but Paul was stoned outside the city and left by the roadside to die. Fortunately he was not too severely hurt and he was able to continue with the tour.

In all these places small Christian churches came into existence, with a mixed membership of Jews and Gentiles. They were warned to abandon their idols and their wine cups, to live soberly, to work for their living, and to seek first the Kingdom of God and his righteousness. The Christian commandments were summed up in loving: love God and love your neighbor. If they did so, they would almost certainly become the butt for neighbors' jokes and perhaps the victims of evil hands, but for such suffering they must be prepared. Let them pray as Jesus had taught his disciples to pray; let them watch, for the final crisis of the world would come like a thief in the night.

At length the missionaries turned on their tracks, revisiting their converts and encouraging the churches, till they came to Attalia, whence they sailed home, tired but triumphant, to Syrian Antioch. When the full story of the mission had been told, the church was at once exuberant with joy and awed at the wonder of it all. It felt that the hand of God had been laid upon it and its missionaries, and the Christians saw with what leaps and bounds the Kingdom was coming with power on the earth.

The news that Barnabas and Paul had admitted Gentiles to full membership in the Church without requiring circumcision spread rapidly among the older churches of Palestine, and in Jerusalem it provoked disquiet and alarm. Some extremists there feared anything that implied a final break with Judaism. The effective leader of the church in Jerusalem for some years had been James the Just, the brother of Jesus, but Peter had returned to the city and his counsel was available. James tended to be a cautious Christian, a diligent attender at Temple and synagogue, a man who did not seem to share the missionary passion of Paul and Peter; yet men respected his judgment and remembered his relationship to Jesus.

Obviously a crisis had arisen and Antioch, the mother church of the mission, resolved to confer with Jerusalem, the mother church of them all. The delegates were Barnabas and Paul, who took with them an uncircumcised Gentile convert called Titus.

Paul's version of this momentous conference was given some six years later in a letter to the churches of Galatia, and in this he stated that he had gone to Jerusalem, not primarily because he had been sent, but rather because God had revealed to him that it was right to go. "When we arrived, we had first a private discussion with the leaders, to whom I outlined the content of the gospel I was accustomed to preach among the Gentiles. My reason for doing so was to insure that I was not running a vain course." Yet Paul also insisted that his call to preach had not come from any man. "I was appointed to preach by Jesus Christ and by God the Father, who raised him from the dead!"

As a result of this meeting, Titus was accepted as a Christian brother without any request at all for his circumcision.

But suddenly the atmosphere changed, for the extremists raised the whole issue publicly and the matter could not be left where it was. With indignation Paul wrote that these people had spied on him and the other leaders and that they were determined to make slaves out of the Gentile converts. They would have to keep the Jewish law—as if God cared about legal observance or counted men righteous on the ground of their merits! So Paul opposed these false brethren and refused to yield them an inch. They were shortsighted; they were false to the mind of Jesus and the love of God. They simply did not understand the meaning of that grace which pardons the guilty when the guilty pleads that he belongs in faith to the Son of God, who loved him and gave his life for him. Bondage or liberty—that was the issue. A narrow Jewish sect or a universal religion—which was the Christian Church to become? Paul had no doubt of the answer, and his evidence of the spiritual power that had been poured out on uncircumcised Gentile disciples clinched the matter. There was no arguing with local "Pentecosts" that produced lives that were radiant and Christlike. Whatever the legalists might say, Paul's converts were Christians, because the risen Lord lived in them!

The Jerusalem leaders thereupon gave Paul and Barnabas the right hand of fellowship. Nothing was added to Paul's gospel by the so-called leaders. "Actually," he wrote, "I don't care whether they are to be called leaders or not; God certainly pays no attention to rank!" But there was a specific agreement that might have seemed a compromise. From henceforth Barnabas and Paul were to lead the mission to the Gentiles; Peter, as before, was to lead the mission to the Jews. Each was valid and each was necessary. To preserve the unity of the whole Church the leaders from Antioch undertook to arrange for contributions of money from the Gentile churches to aid the poorer church

of Jerusalem. "It was the very thing we were anxious to do,"
said Paul; for those who shared the spiritual blessings of
Israel ought to divide their material blessings for the common good. It was accepted on both sides that the high moral
standards inherited from the synagogue were to be maintained.

The delegates of Antioch returned exultant. Paul's victory had been one of principle. He did not mind if some
converts wanted circumcision. What he was determined to
fight was the imposition of this rite on all believers as a
matter of law.

The first fine flush lasted but a short while. Peter came
north to visit Antioch and, correctly interpreting the spirit
of the recent agreement, shared its life fully. At the Lord's
Supper he ate and drank with the Gentile members. Soon
afterward Christians arrived from Jerusalem, saying that
they were in some sense representatives of James. "James
says that Gentiles must observe the diet rules of the law. . . .
James does not approve of this eating together at the Lord's
Table; the two groups must meet separately. . . . James
says . . ." Thus they went on, these men of the "circumcision
party," as Paul called them. The result was a disruption at
Antioch. Peter gave in; the local Jewish Christians followed
his lead; and even Barnabas sided with them this time on
the matter of principle.

Paul was enraged and publicly rebuked Peter, the Rock
of the Church. "You are not hewing a straight line in this
thing at all!" he cried. "You deny the gospel. If you, a Jew,
can live in Gentile fashion, why do you compel Gentiles to
live like Jews? God reckons men righteous, not because they
keep the law—which they cannot do—but solely through
their faith in the Lord Jesus."

It was all of no avail at this time; the rift was made between the two parties. When it was suggested that Barnabas

and Paul should revisit the younger churches of Phrygia and Galatia, Paul declined. For Barnabas wanted to take John Mark again, and to that Paul could not consent. The upshot was that two missions set out from Syrian Antioch: Barnabas and Mark returned to Cyprus and labored to increase the strength of the churches; Paul with a new companion, Silas, went to Pisidia, and South Galatia. Great was their joy to find how firmly the churches had adhered to the faith and how abundantly they had been blessed. If only they could live in complete devotion to their Lord and in the spirit of brotherly love through the days ahead, they would be enabled to surmount all the crises of their life as Christians! They would then be ready to venture into stranger lands with a courage and enterprise that could not be denied. The cause of the Kingdom was marching on, and they must all be worthy of Him who called them into his service!

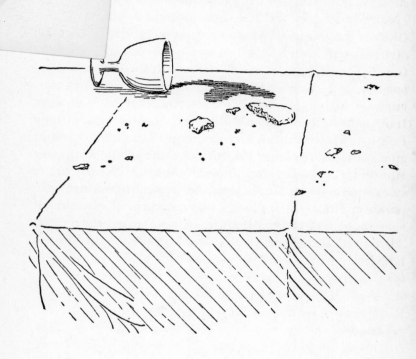

The Problems of a Young Church

14 TWO HUNDRED YEARS before the Christian missions began, Corinth had been a ruined waste, a grim reminder to Greeks that they had lost to the Romans not only political but commercial power as well. Corinth had risen again, thanks to the great Julius Caesar and Augustus, his adopted son, who had settled there Italian ex-slaves, army veterans, landless Greeks, and others. For almost a century it had been a market where Asia and Europe met, since its strategic position gave it ports facing to both worlds.

Corinth was situated on the isthmus at the waist of Greece, with the port of Lechaeum on the west and the port of Cenchreae on the east. From time to time, therefore, Corinthians saw tied up at the docks ships from Spain that had the tang of the Atlantic and of the very ends of the known world in their sails; or ships from Cyrene, Gaul, and Italy manned by motley crews of slaves, Celts and Africans. From Alexandria came the corn ships, for Egypt was the granary of the Empire; others had touched the shores of Rhodes, Miletus, and Cyprus, and some hulls knew even the strange waters beyond the straits at Byzantium on the Bosporus. In their cargoes were silks and spices from the east; Samian pottery; fish and fruits, wines, grain, cloth, and Thyatiran dyes of purple; and always there were slaves, both men and women, highborn and lowborn, the unfortunate victims of war on the Rhine, the Rhone, or even the Thames. Some of these people were offered for sale and found their way into Corinthian homes and shops.

One other group in the mixed population of the city was comprised of Jews: what part of the Roman Empire was without members of this widely dispersed race? The Corinthian Jews were not, however, very wealthy or prosperous and they had many enemies among the Greeks, a witty nation that loved to speculate idly on the deep problems of life. The sailors and stevedores who loaded and unloaded boats by day spent little time on philosophy; by night they sought the city lanes to make the most of those pleasures of wine and women for which Corinth was famous. "Let us eat and drink, for tomorrow we may die!" they sang in a dozen different dialects.

The city could boast a fine open market place and busy shops filled with a variety of merchandise; among the butchers' booths were some that were equipped with running water to keep their meat chilled and fresh. Besides the dignified temples, the theater, the covered arches along the streets, and the dwelling places of rich and poor, Corinth had a tribunal of justice where the proconsul, the deputy of the emperor and senate of Rome, heard cases at law. For new Corinth had been made the capital of the Roman province of Greece, which the Italians called Achaia.

Late in the year 49, Paul of Tarsus, the Jew who was so passionate a follower of Jesus, arrived in Corinth alone and in a state of deep spiritual depression. He had come from Macedonia in the north by way of Athens, after a strenuous and exciting time in the service of the Kingdom of God.

At Lystra in Galatia, during his visit with Silas to the churches founded by Barnabas and himself, Paul had recruited for his personal assistance and for missionary duty a Christian youth called Timothy, the son of a Greek father and a Jewish mother. Then these three, under the guidance of the Spirit of Christ, had made their way to Mysia and the town of Troas. Up to this point the missionaries had encountered, at several stages on their journey, definite barriers to work in other provinces of Asia Minor; but now the way was cleared for them in dramatic fashion. At Troas, Paul dreamed that a Macedonian appealed to him, "Come over and help us!" Believing that it was the will of God, the three men made the momentous decision to take the gospel of the Kingdom over the water to Europe.

In Macedonia they traveled by Roman roads and attempted to establish churches in Philippi, Thessalonica, and Berea. The beginnings were quite hopeful, but in each place the missionaries had to endure sore trials. Silas and Paul were thrown into prison at Philippi and flogged by the authorities; the Jews stirred up strong opposition against them, so that they were driven from pillar to post until finally the converts in Berea decided that it was unsafe for Paul to stay a day longer. They sent him off alone to Athens, where Silas and Timothy would join him later. In the marvelous city of Athens, Paul tried with little success to interest the Greeks in Jesus Christ. When his two friends arrived, they brought disquieting news from Thessalonica, and Paul sent them back at once with a letter to the church there. Meanwhile he himself would remove from the intellectual city of Athens to the commercial center of Corinth and they were to meet him there as soon as possible.

As a craftsman who worked with goat's-hair fabric, Paul quickly found employment with a certain Aquila. This man, with his wife Prisca, had migrated to Corinth from Rome when the emperor Claudius issued an edict expelling all Jews from his capital. Aquila had been able to bring some of his tools and possessions and had set up a leather shop in his new home.

On the Sabbath days Paul and his new friends worshiped in the "Synagogue of the Hebrews," on the Lechaeum road not far from the market. Paul resolved, of course, to preach in this place also his message of the Kingdom and of his Lord; and here the old familiar pattern asserted itself. It seemed impossible to these Greek Jews that the crucified Jesus, whom Paul described so vividly and movingly, could be the long-expected Messiah of their nation who should gather together the scattered children of Abraham. But Paul persevered, and when his colleagues arrived from Thessalonica, he found that he was free to spend all his time on evangelism. Euodia, a Lydian dealer in purple dye at Philippi, and others among the converts of Macedonia had sent Paul gifts of money that made him independent of his trade for many months.

Slowly success became assured: Stephanas and his family

were the first to confess Jesus as Lord and to be baptized by Paul into the Kingdom of divine love. Not long after, Crispus, the chief elder of the synagogue, became a Christian; so did the Gentile Gaius Justus. This made the Corinthian Jews very angry and they formally expelled these Christian "heretics" from their fellowship. Undaunted, Paul and his associates promptly moved into the house of Justus, which was next door to the synagogue, and declared their intention of offering the grace of the Lord Jesus and the power of the Kingdom to the Greeks!

Corinth offered them a large and inviting field. Many strangers who entered by the seaports were sought out and befriended; the poor and lonely welcomed the gospel; slaves who found their life degrading rejoiced to know that they too were invited into the Christian congregation. Among these converts were some who had been the scum of the earth, both Jews and Gentiles; they had been drunkards, robbers, perverts, and worse; they had been parasites on others; they had been cruel and selfish. But now, through the gospel of Jesus, the power of the Kingdom laid hold of them and changed them. Others in the new church had formerly tried to find the meaning of life in the worship of Aphrodite, the goddess of love, whose temple crowned the towering hill, Acrocorinth, under which the city sheltered. Others had frequented the mystery cults among the Syrian and Egyptian immigrants, cults that promised "rebirth into everlasting life." Others again had turned to the alcoholic ecstasies of the worshipers of Dionysus, in the hope that they might escape the cares and sorrows of this life. Now all of them found reality and satisfaction in the good news that initiated them into the Kingdom of everlasting love.

What they heard from the apostles was a true story, not a myth or a mystery. Without any brilliant oratory Paul told them the moving tale of Him who had served the one true God, the Heavenly Father, even to death; who had loved his own even when they had denied him; who had carried the sins of the world and reconciled it to the Father. This Jesus had been highly exalted and given the all-excelling name, God's own name of "Lord." He had risen from the dead and appeared to Peter, to the Eleven, to James, to five hundred or more, and finally to Paul himself. They could check the story from the eyewitnesses! They could see what the power of the Kingdom had done for Paul, the former enemy of the Church! Among those who believed Paul's message, vices were halted and new virtues began to grow. Their faith in Jesus opened their hearts to the coming of the Holy Spirit and raised them into a new fellowship of loving men and women. Aquila and Prisca became convinced of the truth of the gospel. Fortunatus, Achaicus, and Stephanas were elected elders, and the church prospered greatly.

About a year passed and then a new proconsul arrived in Corinth. He was Gallio, the brother of a distinguished Roman philosopher. The leaders of the Jewish synagogue judged this to be an opportune moment to take their case against the Christians to the civil authority. They accused Paul of persuading Jews to serve God contrary to the law of Moses. "I don't know what you are talking about," replied Gallio, "and I couldn't care less. It's nothing but a matter of words and names. Be off with you! I won't be a judge in anything that has to do with your religion—take care of it yourselves!" In the resulting confusion, Sosthenes, the new chief elder of the synagogue, was beaten up; but the uninterested proconsul paid no attention even to a riot.

Shortly afterward Paul decided that he must return to Syrian Antioch, to report on his European missions. Prisca and Aquila, both endowed with rare spiritual gifts and among the apostle's most intimate friends, decided to sail with him from Cenchreae. It was their intention to open a branch of the business in Ephesus, the capital of Asia Minor; and they invited Paul to come soon to preach the Kingdom in that city.

During the next three or four years the young church in Corinth, deprived of Paul's presence, continued to grow but it found many problems on its hands. There were converts who thought that, because they had found fellowship with God through Jesus and had received the Holy Spirit, they were all at once perfect. "We've got our heart's desire already!" they announced. "Haven't we entered into the Kingdom? If the Kingdom has come among us with power, then we are enjoying the blessedness of heaven here!" Such views led to different errors. Some asserted that Paul's teaching meant that the law of Moses had ceased to have any authority; therefore the Ten Commandments need not be observed! They wanted to do as they pleased: so one man took his father's wife as his own. Some got drunk at the Lord's Supper; they were haughty and had no thought for the poor and weak. On the other hand, some of those who felt most "spiritual" declared that they should have nothing to do with the things of the flesh; and among them a few couples lived together as "spiritual brides and grooms," without fulfilling the marriage relationship. Such divisions were very harmful to the church and its reputation.

The Christians of Corinth were surrounded on all sides by pagan ways and pagan influences. If they bought meat in the shops, they might be purchasing what had been dedicated to idols: could they lawfully eat such meat? What should one do at private dinner parties in the homes of non-Christian friends? Women who had pagan husbands, and men whose wives refused to accept Christ, wanted to know if they should divorce the unbelieving partners. A letter from Paul that was read to the church included advice "not to associate with immoral people," and this was taken to mean that Christians should avoid all contacts with outsiders.

Even at worship the spirituality of these enthusiasts produced terrible results. They were always falling into ecstasy: one wanted to sing while another tried to read a lesson; men and women prophesied without controlling their feelings in any way, and often what they said could not be understood by their neighbors. Worship became pandemonium. The Jewish members were shocked by the daring freedom of Christian women who insisted that they too had received the Spirit of God and should be allowed to take part in the service; in the synagogue, women remained quietly and submissively in the gallery! What was to be the rule in the Christian ecclesia? What had Jesus said?

Paul, their father in God, was meanwhile in Ephesus where another church was rapidly assembling, with Prisca and Aquila at its heart. These two had wasted no time in proclaiming the Kingdom of God in the name of Jesus. A learned young teacher, previously a follower of John the Baptist, received instruction from them and was converted. This was Apollos, whom they sent to Corinth, where he had outstanding success in arguments with the Jews. A party of Corinthian Christians professed to find Apollos a better teacher than Paul himself and began to slander the apostle. Paul's friends resisted this; while others, newly come to the city, asserted that Christians should look for leadership to Peter.

All this was reported to Paul from the church in Corinth by Chloe and members of her family; then a delegation arrived in Ephesus to seek his counsel. Paul's answer to the difficulties of Corinth was sent in the form of a lengthy letter to the church. Lovingly and diplomatically he acknowledged the extraordinary gifts poured out on its members by the divine Spirit, but he reminded them that wisdom and love were two of the greatest gifts: Corinth had shown little common sense thus far and did not understand the Christian meaning of love. In Christ they must be united; Christ alone was their Rock and Foundation; was Christ divided? Did they not realize that in Corinth they were "the body of Christ," spiritually joined to him like a bride united with her husband?

They must never equate love with the sensual delights that Aphrodite, the pagan goddess of love, encouraged. Love was what the Lord Jesus had shown, who had yielded his life in self-sacrifice. All the eloquence in the world, generosity without stint, prophecy, the faith that moves mountains—all without that highest form of love—was as good as nothing. Genuine love "is very patient and kind, willing to accept wrongs. It abhors pride and boasting. It is never petulant and childish, not easily provoked to anger; it is always ready to forgive and wants to carry the burdens of others. Faith, hope, and love abide; but the greatest of these is love."

They had sent Paul specific questions and he reminded them that he could instruct his congregations according to the mind of Christ, which was revealed to him by the Spirit. But spiritual truth demanded spiritual understanding!

Yes, they might get married, if they had to; but it was better to do as Paul himself did and stay single in view of the crisis of the times they lived in. It was permissible for Christians to live together without having intercourse, but it was highly dangerous. A widow could certainly remarry, and her second husband should be a believer. Jesus had not approved of divorce and that rule still held. Paul's opinion regarding the difficult situation at Corinth was that members of the church should continue to live with pagan partners as long as possible for the children's sake. After all, they might even convert their wives or husbands! Nevertheless, realities must be faced. If a pagan refused to accept such an arrangement, then the Christian spouse had to separate and the home would be broken up. Some such limitations in the case of mixed marriages were inevitable.

Paul went on to enunciate the rule that he laid down in all his churches: Believers must continue to lead the life they were living when God called them into the fellowship of Christ. It did not matter in the least whether a man was circumcised or not; what did matter was his obedience to the commandments of God. This applied also to slaves. If they had the chance to receive their freedom, well and good; they should take it. But every Christian was the "slave" of the Lord, and everyone who was a slave became spiritually a "freedman" in the Church of the Lord. This teaching was intended to prevent too hasty attempts to change the existing order of political and economic life; Paul considered that Christians were living in "days of waiting," at the end of which the Lord Jesus Christ would be revealed in all the glory of his Kingdom. His followers were to spend these days patiently by learning to live the blessed life of love.

On the subject of women in church the apostle recommended the Jewish practice: they should be veiled, and they were to be quiet at meetings.

What about "food that had been offered to idols"? He admitted that Christians knew very well how foolish it was to think that the gods and goddesses represented by idols really existed! Yet there were weaker brethren who had scruples on this question. His own practice therefore was never to eat anything that might cause offense to others. Those who claimed to be "enlightened" should remember their obligations to their fellow members in the church.

Similarly, at the Lord's Supper, greed and drunkenness were disgraceful. Could they not see that the broken bread recalled the broken body of Christ on the cross and that, by sharing one loaf at the sacrament, the congregation became "the body of Christ"? All of them had gifts, for the common good; some were apostles, some prophets, some teachers; there were others with different functions, but surely all of them were essential to the life and efficiency of the body. So they should honor leaders like Stephanas and help one another.

Paul had given them the gospel free of charge, but only because the Macedonians had made it possible. The Lord Jesus himself had instructed that preachers had a right to live by their preaching.

They had asked when the end would come. Would there be a general resurrection? "Christ will come suddenly," was the reply, "and the dead will rise with him, not as 'flesh and blood,' for that cannot inherit the Kingdom of God. In the new life of eternity believers will have a new 'spiritual' body, an organism adequate for new conditions."

The letter requested them to put aside each week freewill gifts of money to help the church in Jerusalem. Paul planned to stay in Ephesus until Pentecost, for there was much to do. "Then I hope to visit Macedonia, and I would like to spend the winter with you in Corinth. Timothy comes as my personal representative; please make him feel at home among you. Apollos will come, God willing, when he can find time. The grace of the Lord Jesus be with you. I send you my love, in the fellowship of Christ. And I have written this greeting with my own hand."

It might have been expected that such a letter would bring the Corinthians to their senses. But it did not, mainly because one individual stubbornly refused to recognize Paul's spiritual authority. Matters went from bad to worse, until Paul decided that he must go in person and try to set things right.

This visit was extremely painful and humiliating, for he was mocked and contradicted at every turn. His opponent managed to prevent any decisions favorable to Paul's views, and the apostle had to leave without accomplishing anything. Once more he fell into deepest depression: was his work after all to be in vain? Was his own salvation perhaps in jeopardy? He had persecuted the Church, he was proud, he did not always keep his temper in check, he had been bitter against the Jewish extremists at Antioch and elsewhere. Was he to preach the gospel, but himself be a castaway? Had God rejected him? On his return to Ephesus dear friends like Prisca, Rufus and his mother, Urbanus and Stachys, and the beloved Persis, as well as his two colleagues, Silas and Timothy, did everything they knew to comfort him. Then new troubles crowded upon him: word came from Galatia, Corinth, and Philippi that the Jewish extremists were trying to undo his work; they were preaching a different Jesus and a different gospel. ("Cursed be anyone who does this, even if it be an angel straight from heaven!" he wrote to the Galatians.) In Ephesus itself enemies made his life such a misery that he was ready for death to come and end it all.

To deal with the problem of Corinth he composed another letter, which he sent by Timothy. It was a bitter attack on the opponent who was slandering his good name and ridiculing his personality: "Paul is the kind of weakling who browbeats you with letters, but his case collapses when he has to meet you face to face. . . . Paul has no delivery and compares ill with our Greek orators. . . . Where are his credentials as an apostle? Can he stand up beside our friends from Jerusalem?"

"Oh, I am mad to do this!" wrote Paul with passion, "but

you force me to it. Have these false apostles something to
show? So have I! I am a true Jew descended from Abraham;
I have suffered for the faith over and over again—beaten in
the synagogue, flogged by the Romans, stoned, shipwrecked,
thrown into prison. My whole life has spelled danger:
danger by sea and land, by road and river, in town and
desert, from Jews and Gentiles! Can your false apostles
produce signs and wonders? I must not boast, but I could
tell you of a man who was caught up into paradise and
heard things it is unlawful to mention. What fools you are
not to know that even Satan masquerades as an angel of
light! Look here: I am all set to visit you for the third time,
and I repeat the warning I gave you last time. If I do
come, I will spare no one. We shall see whether my Christ
acts only in words or in deeds of power."

What response would Corinth make to a document so
peremptory? He could not wait to hear: Titus must go to
Corinth. Titus must tell them again that Paul loved them
with all his heart and suffered agonies in their behalf. Paul
would make his way to Troas and meet his brother there.
Meanwhile, there was no news from Timothy; and at Troas,
when he got there, Titus was not to be found. The Christians at Troas wanted him to stay with them, for there was
much he could do; but with cares and sorrows beating on
him, he was too wretched and restless. All that mattered was
the news from Corinth, and he would cross to Macedonia
in the hope that he would hear there what he was so pathet-
ically anxious to hear.

In Corinth, Titus found that the letter had caused pain
and grief; it had achieved nothing, and Timothy was getting nowhere. Calmly and lovingly Titus fulfilled his commission, congratulating the Corinthians on their wonderful
possibilities for the service of the Kingdom of God in
Greece. He described for them the tears and distress of

Paul as he wrote the letter that caused them pain. If they professed the love of Jesus, they must obey the commandments of Jesus. Paul coveted nothing but their welfare, their growth in wisdom, their happiness.

To the arguments of Titus, Corinth responded with a strong revulsion of feeling in Paul's favor; they censured his opponent with the utmost severity and threatened him with such dreadful penalties that the man feared for his life. Titus was requested to hurry north and tell Paul how eagerly the church longed to see him again.

For the time being good sense had prevailed, and the Corinthians settled down to a more sober religion. They had begun to understand that the kind of life appropriate to the Kingdom of God consisted in loving one another, and that loving involved self-discipline and self-sacrifice. Moreover, they had learned from Paul that the Church throughout the world was one, a family or a brotherhood, "the body of Christ." Admittedly, their situation in a place like Corinth was difficult and perplexing; but wisdom, no less than joy or enthusiasm, was a gift of the Spirit. They knew now that they must fight the good fight of faith, trusting that He who had called them into his Kingdom would continually be their aid and their defense.

The Sons of the
Kingdom Must Suffer

15 SEATED among the elders of the church in Philippi,
Clement was listening intently to the letter from
Paul the apostle that was being read to the assembled mem-
bership.

"I beg Euodia and I beg Syntyche to be of one mind as
Christians; yes, and I would ask you, my trusty Zyzygos,
to help these women. They were fellow athletes

with Clement and myself and the rest of my colleagues in the contest for the gospel; and the names of my fellow workers are written in the book of life."

Clement! Paul had singled him out for special mention; he had never forgotten his friends!

Ah, but how could any of them in Philippi forget their beloved apostle? Euodia, the lady from Thyatira in the Asia Minor district of Lydia, had been the first Christian in the colony. Clement had heard the story often: with others of Euodia's household she had met Paul and his party at the Jewish place of prayer beside the river, and not long afterward she had committed herself to the faith that Jesus was the Christ and the redeemer from sins. Paul had baptized her and welcomed her into the Church of God. The Lydian then invited Paul and his companions to stay in her large house, and they had gratefully accepted.

Those had been exciting days in Macedonia, and Paul had talked of turning Philippi, which was a colony of Rome, into a colony of God's Kingdom! Most of the Jews, like the Jews throughout the Empire, had rejected the good news and had made a lot of trouble. Before long Silas and Paul found themselves in prison without a trial, on accusations by the pagan masters of a slave girl out of whom Paul had cast an evil spirit. Paul was always in prison or in trouble of some sort! It had been well said, thought Clement, that the sons of the Kingdom must suffer.

Their Jewish and Greek opponents had made life very hard for the struggling church after Paul's departure, and like other young congregations they had had their own internal contentions and discords. Some of their women, just like the Lydian Euodia and Syntyche, had quarreled over trifles. On the whole, however, Clement said to himself, the Philippians had held fast to the truth; they had honestly been happy that they were Christian enough to arouse the antagonism of evil men. For Christ's sake and the Kingdom's they would suffer the loss of many things.

It was already four years more or less, Clement calculated, since they had last seen their beloved founder; and then he had slipped in secretly.

When the troubles in Corinth were over and his personal prestige restored, Paul had eventually traveled south to visit that fickle church at the isthmus. He had spent most of a winter with the Corinthians and laid plans for his next great missionary enterprise. Clement recalled with what astonishment some of the Philippians had listened as Paul told them about the project: to proclaim the Kingdom of God in Spain on the far western frontier of the Empire, and to visit the Christians of Rome on the way! What an imperial imagination the man had! He was resolved that all the kingdoms of this world should become the Kingdom of our God, the Father, and of Jesus Christ, the image and Son of the Father! It seemed as if the powers of the Holy Spirit of God were focused on the apostle's heart and mind for the sole purpose of saving and reconciling the whole world of mankind.

In Corinth, Paul had finally made up his mind that, before he could adventure in the west, he would go to Jerusalem with the delegates of the Gentile congregations, to deliver their generous contributions for the support of the church in the Holy City. "What I really hope for," Paul had told them, "is that I may be able to allay once and for all the suspicions of these fanatical Jewish Christians who have been dogging my steps at every turn, trying to subvert my people." The original proposal had been that Paul would sail directly from Cenchreae, but at the last minute a plot of the Corinthian Jews to murder Paul on the road to the seaport was discovered, and as a result the apostle had journeyed secretly by the overland route to Macedonia.

The Philippians had been overjoyed to see him again, if only for a few days; then they had said good-by to him and to their dear friend Luke the physician. Luke had gone with Paul to Troas and Palestine, and even now he was in Rome too.

"Give my greetings to your church members, united with me in Christ Jesus. The brethren who are beside me send their greetings to you; in fact, all the Christians here do. But the slaves who are in the emperor's palaces wish specially to be remembered to you."

The reader was almost at an end, and Clement's mind reviewed in a flash the rest of Paul's journey to Jerusalem and to Rome. He had reached Palestine safely, after meeting with many of his faithful friends on the way. In Jerusalem he had been cautiously received. Then some informers falsely accused him of taking uncircumcised Gentiles into the Temple unlawfully. Presumably he had done so on the ground that, as Christians, such people now had the right of going past the Court of the Gentiles into the courts reserved for the holy people of God. It was undoubtedly a pack of lies, but the Jewish mob had not waited to find out the facts. They were dragging him outside the city walls to stone him like another Stephen, when the Romans arrested him on the suspicion that he was a long-wanted criminal. Ever since, Paul had been in Roman custody; first in Jerusalem, then in Caesarea, and now in the "Eternal City" itself. Governor after governor had hesitated to become embroiled in what seemed to be a mad Jewish dispute about a man who had risen from the dead. At last, in desperation, Paul had cried out to Festus, the procurator in charge of Judea: "If I am a criminal, let my accusers state their case in due form and I will abide by a proper decision. I am a Roman and I claim the rights and privileges of a citizen. I stand at Caesar's tribunal and I appeal to Caesar!"

"You have appealed to Caesar," said Festus; "then to Caesar you shall go!"

All this the Philippians knew from letters that Luke had sent.

After a long and stormy voyage, during which their ship was wrecked off the island of Malta, Paul and those who had been permitted to go with him had reached Rome. Month followed month and still there had been no decision in his case. The authorities were lenient enough. Paul was allowed to take lodgings and, under surveillance, receive inquirers and friends. How could he be guilty before his offense had been adequately defined and proved? Everyone knew that the business about defiling the Temple of the Jews, for which the penalty under Jewish law was death, was merely a trumped-up charge. His enemies in Jerusalem simply wanted to be rid of the most influential Christian "heretic." But what did the emperor Nero understand about the difference between Jews and Jewish Christians? or about the vexed problem of admitting Gentiles to the Church of God without first making them Jews by religion?

Philippi and all the churches of the Pauline mission field had been kept informed about the conditions under which Paul was living and working in Rome. The Philippians, the readiest to share his tribulations, had therefore sent one of their own elders (whom as Greeks they also called "bishops") with gifts of money for his assistance; and this man, Epaphroditus, was instructed to stay in Rome as long as he could in order to serve their apostle.

And here was Epaphroditus come home again, looking like a man who had returned from the grave!

Clement heard with immense interest the story that his fellow bishop was telling the congregation; for the letter had been read in full.

It was perfectly true, he told them, that he had been so

ill that he lay at death's door for some days. Everyone had despaired of his life, but, thanks to the infinite goodness of God and in answer to their prayers, he had recovered.

He had found Paul quite well, despite all his hardships; and still the same in respect to his fierce, dynamic energy. The service of the Kingdom and the care of all his churches, however, had taken toll of the apostle; his hair was much thinned and he had aged a lot. The Philippians knew as well as any that Paul's body carried the weals and scars of many a battle, many a flogging in the synagogues, many exposures to sea and wind and rain. Paul was accustomed to call them the marks of his enslavement to Jesus Christ, his Master: "I am branded for Christ's sake!"

They said to Epaphroditus, "What did Paul mean when he wrote in this letter, 'He risked his life to make up for your services . . . receive him with Christian fellowship and joy, and honor men like him'?" Epaphroditus was reluctant to speak; he suggested that Paul had been exaggerating any kindness that he had been able to do for him. Finally, for they pressed him, he admitted that he had volunteered for some dangerous missions in Rome. The emperor Nero was a madman, and things were going from bad to worse. His spies had been everywhere, and Paul had heard that some Jews and even some Jewish Christians were in contact with them. Naturally Paul feared for his life, and Epaphroditus had tried to find out what was going on in the synagogues and in the tenements where most of the Jews lived down by the river Tiber.

"So that was what Paul referred to at the beginning of the letter?" someone asked. "Let's hear that part again."

" 'I should like you to know, brethren,' " read the bishop, 'that things have actually turned out to the advantage of the gospel here. In the praetorian palace it is known that I am a prisoner simply because I am a Christian. Now many of the Christians here have taken heart and are preaching more boldly. It is true that some are preaching Christ in a spirit of jealousy, thinking to do me an ill turn while I languish in jail .... What does it matter? One way or another Christ is being preached, and I'm glad of it!' "

He is glad of that, they said to each other with amazement; why, his whole letter is full of joy and love!

They were quite right. Paul reminded them that they should deal with one another in the same way that God had dealt with them in Christ. What a Lord was theirs who had humbled himself to suffer death even on a cross, he who was 'the image of God'! It was for this that God also had highly exalted him so that, at the name of Jesus, every knee in earth and heaven should bow. He was their example: they were to shine in a dark world like the stars in the night sky. They were to live in joy always, for the believer had gladness in his heart; they must continue unweariedly in prayer. "Fill your minds," wrote the apostle, "with everything that is true, honorable, just, and pure; with everything that is lovely and gracious. If there be anything that deserves to be praised, any excellence, think on these things. Follow my example: do the things that you have learned from me, or received from me; do what you have heard from me and observed in me. For then God will bless you with his peace."

In his letter Paul also told them how much he appreciated their kindnesses to him from the earliest days of their church until now. When Christ was revealed in glory, their apostle would be proud of them; provided they ran the race of the Christian life so as to win the crown. Their whole life should be like a sacrificial offering to God; and Paul would be well content if his own lifeblood had to be poured out to make theirs fully adequate. Actually, he was in two minds about the future: was death preferable to life? To go on living in this world might mean helping them, and that would give him joy. But he had a deep longing in his heart to depart and thus to be with Christ, for nothing could be better than that. "Christ means life to me!"

"Rejoice, therefore!" he wrote. "Rejoice! I will repeat that word over and over again."

Clement found the tears springing to his eyes, and when he looked about him he found that there was scarcely a dry eye in the whole congregation. They were all thinking of the implications in what Epaphroditus had said: The emperor was a madman, and things were going from bad to worse.

It wasn't only in Philippi that Christian men and women were waiting for the news out of Rome.

At Colossae in Asia Minor, a town several miles inland from Ephesus, another companion of Paul had arrived with a letter from his Roman prison. Tychicus had been invited one day to see the prisoner, who told him that he was to return to the east for two reasons.

In the first place, it was reported from Colossae that strange teachings and novel practices were being promoted in that church. Apparently some new teachers were suggesting that Christ was not enough. There was much more to the revelation of God than could be found in Jesus Christ! Paul had written to show the Colossians that Christ is the Son, "the image of the invisible God: in him we have the fullness of the Godhead in bodily form. In Christ and him alone do we begin to see how to make sense of the whole universe. Through him we learn that the creation is good and that the God of love has a purpose for it. Thank God, then, that he has removed us into the Kingdom of his well-beloved Son!" Tychicus was to instruct them further in the message of Paul's gospel and help them to be obedient to Jesus and his precepts of love. That obedience would certainly not be effected by observing legalistic regulations about Jewish Sabbaths or new moon festivals or by the ascetic practices advocated by the heretical teachers among the Colossians. "I have put in a special message to Archippus," Paul told his friend, "telling him to fulfill his ministry. Help him! Stay as long as you think necessary, and don't worry about me: God will take care of me! Build up the church in the traditions it learned from Epaphras when he evangelized them at the first."

Tychicus took careful note of these instructions.

Next Paul told him that he was to escort to Laodicea, which was on his route, the slave boy Onesimus, who had run away from his master Philemon and come to Rome; there he had found Paul and become a Christian, helping Paul in all sorts of ways and endearing himself to everyone.

Onesimus did not want to go, and he wept bitterly at the parting from one whom he might never see again. Paul was very firm and sent them off. To the slave he entrusted a short personal letter to Philemon, his wife Apphia, and his son Archippus.

Now, several weeks later, Philemon was gazing in astonishment at the runaway and had the apostle's letter in his hand:

"Paul, Christ's ambassador and now also a prisoner for his sake, appeals to you for my son, Onesimus, on the ground of love." (Philemon raised his eyebrows at that word "son"!) "I became his 'father' in my prison and I have sent him back to you. It is true he was a 'useless' character with you and not an 'Onesimus' at all; but I certify that he is 'useful' nowadays both to you and to me! Parting with him means parting with my very heart. I could have kept him as your substitute, for you owe me your soul; but I wanted you to act entirely of your own free will. Charge to my account any wrong he did you and accept my personal guarantee: 'With my own hand I write that I, Paul, will repay it.'"

By this time the heart of Philemon had been moved to tears at the thought of his dear master writing like this under the very shadow of death; with such gentle humor requiring Philemon's soul, and clearly expecting that Onesimus would be sent back to him.

"Greetings to you all," Paul ended, "from Epaphras, my fellow prisoner; and from my colleagues Mark, Aristarchus, Demas, and Luke. The grace of the Lord Jesus Christ bless your spirit!"

How could any Christian refuse such a writer? Onesimus was welcomed by the whole family as a long lost brother in Christ and the return of the prodigal was celebrated with great joy. It was all equally overwhelming to the slave. When Philemon and his son told him that he would receive his freedom just as soon as it could be arranged, his cup of happiness, already full, was filled to overflowing. "Then you must return to Paul in Rome, for Paul is in danger and he needs you most," they said to him. Tychicus had told the Laodiceans that the emperor Nero was a madman, and that things were going from bad to worse. What might already have happened, they did not dare to contemplate.

Onesimus told his friends all that he knew about Paul's plight and his chances of escaping death. He told them how, to the joy of all of them who had the unity of the churches at heart, John Mark, the kinsman of Barnabas, had rejoined the apostle. Nevertheless, Mark and Joshua Justus were the only Jewish Christians assisting Paul in the service of the Kingdom of God. Luke, Paul's beloved doctor, was still with him and, as always, was proving himself a tower of strength. Timothy, whose name was associated with Paul's in the letters to the Colossians and to Philemon, was the unfailing friend and spiritual son who had been through much suffering with Paul. Timothy would never desert his teacher and friend.

It was a very tired lad who went to bed that night in the old home, conscious of the tremendous transformation that had been wrought in his own life and in the life of his master's family. Here was one who had been a slave in this house, who had robbed them and run away, accepted in Jesus' name as an honored guest and brother! He went to sleep at last, his mind full of plans for the journey he must soon make once more, back to Paul, back to Rome . . . to Rome.

In Rome, as the weeks and months had passed, the government of the emperor Nero had indeed gone from bad to worse. Once the pupil of Seneca the Stoic philosopher, once a ruler from whom much had been expected, Nero had become the cruelest, maddest, most feared of all tyrants; a monster who had killed his own mother! He treated Rome as if it were his playground and the Empire as a private estate that was to feed his lust and gluttony. As orgy followed orgy, none knew where the assassin's knife would strike next; and even men like Seneca had been driven to suicide in order to escape him.

Rome had no defense against him. It was a proud and ancient city that had won the greatest power in the world almost by chance, for at first its rulers had not coveted land in the east or west of the Mediterranean. Situated on its seven hills, it was called the Eternal City, the mistress of the nations. Its parks and villas were magnificent; its temples, colonnades, and public buildings were decorated with many kinds of scented wood, with bronze, iron, gold, and marble that sparkled in the sun. From the Forum of Rome broad roads led to every part of the world, with signs pointing east to Jerusalem and west to London, a small garrison town in the land of the Britons. It was a city of millions: rich and poor, Syrians and Egyptians, Jews and Spaniards, Gauls and Africans, Greeks and Italians. Artists, poets, writers, orators, and teachers all flocked to it, the center of their universe. Emperors and wealthy patrons competed for the favor of the mobs with games in the circus, lavish processions, and free doles of grain.

But, in spite of all this grandeur and the high and ancient traditions of the past, Rome was built on sand so far as the character of its citizens was concerned. Cruelty was common. Baby girls were thrown out to die. The best of the Romans complained that old-fashioned virtues and piety toward the gods of the fathers were dying out. Wars had destroyed the faith of thousands, who believed that life meant nothing and that there was no future after death.

It was little wonder that many who were worried and afraid of death tried the exotic Oriental cults from Syria, Egypt, and Greece; and that even the synagogues of the Jews attracted Romans, poor and noble alike.

Nero and his government had their eye on the Jews, a people that always could be counted on to resist the tyranny of conquerors; but the Jews for their part had influence of the highest order in the court of the emperor. It was well known to the authorities that the Jewish community in Rome had recently been much disturbed, and they found out that this internal discord was somehow connected with their own problem prisoner, Paul of Tarsus. Paul was a Jew of a queer sort, for he claimed to serve someone called Jesus, or the Christ, who was a Jewish king no longer alive. Another Jew of the same persuasion and also a notable leader had arrived in the city in the past few weeks, a man called Simon Peter. In the provinces there had been several clashes between the strict Jews and these Christian Jews. What the difference between them was remained something of a mystery to the government.

Nero was going from bad to worse, and Rome lay in uneasy anticipation of doom. The police had orders to have criminals ready on whom the emperor could throw the blame for arson or riot or murder, if the necessity arose. For Nero himself did not know what he might do to proud Rome in one of the drunken rages that maddened him or in one of his fiendish frolics. Underground sources suggested to the police that the Christians might prove suitable victims for this purpose. They were unsociable "atheists," who refused to worship the Roman gods and who preached instead a divine Kingdom, acknowledging another Lord besides the emperor. Other contacts among the Jews and Jewish Christians themselves let it be known that they did not trust Paul of Tarsus, of whom they were curiously jealous. He was splitting the Jewish nation, they asserted, and any civil war among the Jews would quickly prove a menace to the peace and prosperity of the whole Empire. Paul should be carefully watched at any rate!

The results of this envy and dissension were immediate. If scapegoats were wanted for some final madness of Nero, here were the people: this Paul, the treasonable preacher of a Kingdom of God that competed with the kingdom of Caesar; this Peter, a preacher of the same divine Kingdom and of a Jewish God who would brook no rivals; and the disciples of these two men, the renegade Jews, the renegade Romans, and others who assembled secretly by night to bind themselves by the oath of their sacrament to the Christ who had died. Let them look out! Let them be prepared to suffer, these sons of the Kingdom. Swords and crosses were in ample supply!

Suddenly Paul was deprived of his limited freedom, and the group about him was scattered. One day a strong military guard came to his lodging and seized him. He was not allowed to bid his friends farewell: the fewer people he saw, the better! He could make no arrangements about his few possessions: he would need nothing where he was going!

"Off with him; watch him carefully; he is a dangerous fellow."

When the Christians at last discovered where Paul had been taken, they learned that he had been dropped into the darkest dungeons of the Mamertine prison. And everyone knew that no man ever emerged from that place alive.

The Household of Faith

16 WHEREVER JEWS GATHERED throughout the Greco-Roman world in the fateful year 70, their one source of conversation was the awful calamity that had befallen their fellow countrymen in Jerusalem and Judea. Fanatical nationalists had revolted against the majesty and might of the Roman Empire in the hope that they might win freedom. Prophets and teachers had promised them that someday God's Messiah would appear among them and lead them to victories far surpassing any of the past; they would become again a glorious people to whom their enemies would bow in subjection. The whole history of the nation, with its extraordinary capacity for rising from the dead, inspired them to take the sword. The example of the Maccabees, two centuries before, was held before their eyes, so that nothing seemed impossible. "To arms!" their leaders called. "For the covenant and the Lord: To arms! Rebel! Destroy the Gentile oppressor!"

Across the hills of Judea and north to the fertile land of Galilee sounded the summons to war.

But Rome had not been caught unready. Vespasian, the commanding general on the eastern frontier, marched against the rebels and defeated them. Soon he had shut them up in the fortress of Jerusalem. Then he was acclaimed by his men as a new emperor, and he departed for Rome to seize the throne. His son Titus completed the conquest, and the most dreadful sufferings were imposed on the nation.

Jerusalem itself was pillaged and razed to the ground. Just as Jesus had foretold, the proud, magnificent Temple lay in ruins and the shock of this event etched itself on the heart and imagination of every Jew, both in the homeland and in the Dispersion. The loss of this holy shrine was unforgettable. It meant that no sacrifices could any more be offered there; and by the law of Moses no alternative altar was permitted at which the priests and Levites could praise the Lord, plead for the nation, and offer the due sacrifices for the sins of priests and people alike. It was a deathblow at the heart of the Jewish religion, blotting out many a fair hope, plunging all Israel into mourning. Rome could be relied on to take no chances of such a rebellion in the future. Everywhere was desolation and wailing. They had neither Kingdom nor Messiah; there was only the quiet of grass growing over dead men's graves; only the silence of heaven.

And yet the religion of Judaism went on; the Jews refused to abandon hope.

If a man traveled in Syria and Asia Minor, in Egypt and Babylon, and even in Rome itself, he would find colonies of faithful worshipers gathering each Sabbath in their synagogues.

This was a miracle of piety and endurance. None but a few Jews could be persuaded to give up their ancestral faith for the worship of Greek or Syrian or Italian gods. No one would admit that this was the end of Israel as a nation and a holy people, however desperate the situation might be. It was better to put the blame on themselves and accept the loss of the Temple and all their sufferings as the punishment of the Lord for their own disobedience. In the long run God would raise them up again, for he was bound to his own promises and to the covenant made with Moses and earlier with Abraham. Israel was still the chosen nation, and its King-Messiah would surely come sometime.

"Even so, come quickly!" they prayed in the synagogues.

There was another body of men and women who were equally dispersed in that Roman world. They too believed in God, the living God who had blessed Abraham, Moses, and others in Israel. But they had found new peace and joy in the certainty that God's Messiah had already come. Jesus was the Christ, the true Lord of all mankind, the King who reigned in love over his disciples. In Jesus, God had already set his Kingdom in the world, as he had promised, and by his gracious providence it was growing everywhere in the most wonderful way.

This Christian Dispersion, like the Jewish, had become accustomed to persecution and death, sorrow and separation. For, paradoxical as it seemed, it was in this way that the Kingdom of God grew. Through their communities from east to west, from the borders of Illyricum to the North African deserts, beyond Damascus, and in the heart of Alexandria spread news of courage and hope. Nero, the mad emperor, had set his capital on fire and made the Christians his scapegoats. Paul had been executed, Peter crucified, and hundreds martyred in the cruel fires. Everywhere the same message resounded in the churches: "Carry on the traditions of Peter and Paul! Follow their example as they followed Jesus our Lord; give yourselves to the work of God's Kingdom, remembering the words of the Master: 'Blessed are they who are persecuted for righteousness' sake'!" When they assembled in houses and halls on the Lord's Day, the first day of the week, they said: "This is the day of our glad assurance and hope, because on this day Jesus our Lord conquered death! Jesus is with us still in the power of his Spirit; one day he will take his power and glory, and then he will reign forever and ever! Glory to the Father in heaven!"

"Even so," they prayed in their churches, "come quickly, Lord Jesus!"

Thus in the generation that followed the destruction of Jerusalem and the Christian martyrdoms at Rome, churches and synagogues existed side by side. But as the years went past, they drew farther and farther apart. For the gospel of the cross and the resurrection was taken by traders, slaves, soldiers, sailors, and government officials, as well as missionaries, to the valley of the Nile, to the heart of Italy, to southern France and the borders of Spain. Every conquest of the cross in new lands and every accession of strength in districts already evangelized lessened the proportion of Jews in this mighty movement of the Holy Spirit that was the Church of God, the body of Christ. Few who had watched the intoxicated delight of the first Pentecost in Jerusalem

could have foreseen the length and breadth of this Christian
Dispersion, nor the abundance, in such a short space of
time, of the harvest from the mission of Jesus. Men and
women of diverse races had been re-created by the Spirit of
the Lord, because Christians had obeyed the will of their
Lord by going forth into Jerusalem and Judea, to Samaria,
and even to the uttermost part of the earth, preaching that
Jesus is Lord and bringing the Gentiles of many nations to
offer their lives in the sacrificial service of the Kingdom of
God.

As these years passed, the membership of the churches
was increased also by the young men and women who grew
up in their families. At church and in their homes they
heard about the Christ who had taught in Palestine; they
recalled his dying love whenever they celebrated the sacrament of his Supper; and if traveling prophets and teachers
visited them, they asked for authentic stories about their
Lord and those who had known him. For some considerable
time it was enough for them to hear over and over again
from such teachers what Jesus had said and done; but as the
original disciples died, it became necessary to have written
records to preserve the teaching of the apostles. At Rome,
John Mark composed a new kind of book which told the
story of the Messiah Jesus, and later other men took his book
and added to it from collections of Jesus' parables and instructions. Independently of Mark and these others, an inspired teacher in Ephesus, also called John, wrote a Gospel
that showed how God had spoken his saving word in Jesus,
his well-beloved Son, and how the Holy Spirit had been
given to the disciples after Jesus rose from the dead. Soon
these Gospel books were being used in the weekly services of
worship, and from them many sermons were preached to
guide congregations in their Christian duty.

Some Christians of Jewish descent continued to observe

the Sabbath, but for them all the first day of the week was much more important. At church meetings, very often in the houses of members, they gave thanks to God the Father in the name of Jesus for all his loving-kindness, and for the presence of the Spirit to teach and encourage them in the way of love. "Blessed be the God and Father of our Lord Jesus Christ!" one of the Christian teachers wrote. "By his great mercy we have been called into a new existence, a life of hope, through the resurrection of Jesus Christ from the dead. Our inheritance is imperishable, undefiled, and unfading, for it belongs to the realm of heaven. At the end of the ages it is going to be revealed, and in the meantime it is reserved in heaven for us. Hallelujah!"

On the evening of the first day, the Christians gathered at the Lord's Table for that Supper which was his memorial and also the place of his deepest communion with them as a congregation. Only baptized believers were allowed to remain for this part of the meeting, for in this most sacred rite the Church offered a sacrifice of thanksgiving to God. On the holy table stood a loaf and a chalice of wine.

Adoration was the first, as it was the last, note struck in the worship. "Great and wonderful are thy deeds, Lord God Almighty!" the presiding elder might say. "Just and true are thy ways, O King of the nations! Who will not fear and glorify thy name, O Lord? For thou only art holy. All nations will come and worship in thy presence, and we with all the hosts of heaven praise and adore thee, saying, 'Holy, holy, holy is the Lord of Sabaoth; the whole creation is full of thy glory.' Be merciful unto us and bless us, who have fled to thee for refuge through our Lord Jesus Christ, to whom is the glory and the majesty forever and ever." And to this prayer the people responded with the "Amen."

They sang familiar psalms and new Christian songs of the Spirit. Portions of the Law and the Prophets were read from the Old Testament, and one of their teachers explained how in Jesus these prophecies had been fulfilled and more than fulfilled. Words of the Lord Jesus and stories about him were related too, and sometimes the letter of a Christian missionary was read.

With hands upraised, they stood to intercede for the body of Christ throughout the world and for men and women of all sorts and conditions. They prayed for their rulers, that God would guide and overrule those whom he had set over them; for unbelievers, that they might be brought into the light and liberty of the divine Kingdom; for fellow Christians, their brethren in the holy family of God: "Save those who are in affliction, have mercy on the lowly, raise the fallen, heal the sick, bring back those who wander, feed the hungry, ransom our prisoners, strengthen the weak, and comfort the fainthearted. Let all the nations know that thou art God alone, that Jesus Christ is thy Son, and that we are thy people, the sheep of thy pasture." Always and everywhere they blessed God the Father for his wondrous salvation of the world through Jesus Christ. "Give us this day our daily bread," they said, "and nourish us daily with thy Spirit."

At the Table a sermon taught them to seek their peace and joy in the Word of life, Jesus their Lord; and often the preacher would speak to them after the manner of John of Ephesus and his Gospel:

"Let us eat his flesh and drink his blood, so that we may in truth belong to his body. His words and his Spirit unite us to him, for in the Spirit he is constantly present with us. Above all else, let us love one another in deeds, not merely in words; for it was his commandment, 'Love one another as I have loved you.' You remember the story of how, on the night in which he was betrayed, the Lord Jesus took a towel and washed his disciples' feet. We are to follow this example, and serve each other humbly and lovingly. Day by day we should work diligently, not simply to satisfy our employers, but as those who are responsible to God. For in this way we shall be a credit to the gospel and our neighbors will see the Christlike life in us.

"Come now to the Table and feed spiritually on the Christ; he is the Vine, we are the branches. By this we know that we have communion with the Father and the Son: namely, by the power of the Spirit and by the love that God grants to us.

"Let us give thanks," the presiding minister would say.

"We ought in everything to give Him thanks to whom is glory forever and ever. Amen," responded the congregation.

Then in the manner that was customary or, if he were a prophet, in the freedom of the Spirit, the leader expressed the praise of the church for the creation, for salvation in Jesus, and for the whole life of the brotherhood.

Next the bread was broken before them, and the minister repeated the words of Jesus, "This is my body, broken for you." The cup of wine diluted with water was passed round with the word, "This cup is the new covenant in my blood." From the elders and teachers the bread and the cup were passed to the assembly by the deacons in a silence full of awe and of joy. Sometimes men or women, deeply moved by the Holy Spirit, prayed aloud to bless and adore their Heavenly Father, crying, "Abba," whispering, "Amen" or, "Alleluia." But at this stage in the life of the churches ecstatic outbursts were fewer; there was much more self-discipline, for they had come to understand that every gift of the Spirit was meant for the common good. They were the household of faith, one in faith and hope and love. When they said the Lord's Prayer together and gave thanks for the martyrs and all the faithful who had died, they had a still deeper sense of what it meant to be citizens in the Kingdom of God.

At the end of the sacrament they were dismissed with the divine blessing, in the name of the Father and the Son and the Holy Spirit. So they departed into the darkness of the night and into the common round of their daily life, moved and inspired by the consciousness that, beyond the changes and evils of their world, heaven in all its eternal light and security was theirs. They might suffer with their Lord, but they would also reign with him. Nothing could take them from the loving care of God, the God of the resurrection miracle, the God of the everlasting Kingdom of love.

Jesus Shall Reign

17 BY THE TIME the first Christian churches had been in existence fifty or sixty years, all nationalities and kinds of people were represented in their membership, and some of them brought in views about God and his activity that were hard to reconcile with the first proclamations of the gospel. The new generations of young people, who had not been converted from pagan idolatry like their grandfathers or their parents, had a different outlook on life from that of the earliest Jewish Christians in Palestine. They had still to meet, however, the taunts of Jews and the slanders of pagan neighbors just as their predecessors had. The fact that the Lord Jesus had not returned in any visible sense had to be reckoned with, and there were people here and there who complained about this. "Where is the promised Coming?" they asked. If it was asserted that Jesus had inaugurated a new era in history, there were skeptics who wanted to know why evil still flourished; why the rich and powerful oppressed the poor; why honest men were beaten, robbed, and murdered; why so many Christians had to suffer disease, bereavements, accidents, and other troubles.

There was one group of believers who had become slack in their worship and daily life because the expectation of a speedy return of Jesus had grown dim. To them a distinguished teacher sent an exhortation which is known as The Letter to the Hebrews. In this epistle the writer undertook to demonstrate the unique greatness of Jesus as the Son of God and the High Priest of the faithful. Jesus had made once and for all the only sacrifice necessary to reconcile sinful men to God Most Holy. By faith in him men and women could enter the divine presence and receive the blessings of the new covenant. The writer reminded his readers of their glorious past and entreated them to stand fast for Christ, the pioneer and finisher of their faith.

In the neighborhood of Ephesus there were some who claimed to have the Spirit of God, but denied that Jesus was the Son of the Father. "We have *real* knowledge of God," they said. "*We* enjoy fellowship with God the Father, and we are sinless!" John the Elder replied that no teaching could be accepted that did not agree with the traditions handed down from the original apostles; secret knowledge and revelations must be tested by that standard, and men who thought they possessed a divine spirit must face the judgment of those who could truly witness to the Lord Jesus and his message. Any so-called "spirit" that advocated immoral behavior could not possibly be Christian.

John had also to meet the challenge of heretics who professed to believe in "Jesus Christ," but asked with some contempt, "How could eternal God stoop to become man?" Consequently, the man Jesus was not the Christ of God, the eternal Savior. Two explanations of this strange doctrine were being offered: one was that the "Spirit-Christ" had entered Jesus at his baptism and stayed in him temporarily. Just before the crucifixion this "Christ" left the man Jesus to die on the cross; the divine and immortal "Christ" then returned to heaven. The other explanation was that Jesus of Nazareth had not really been a man at all! For the divine Savior, the Christ of God, had manufactured something that looked like a human being; it could walk and talk, laugh and cry, eat and sleep: but it was a mere image of a man. To this the teachers of the Church answered that Peter, James, and John, and the other apostles had lived with Jesus and knew that he was truly a man: the heretics were inventing lies half a century after the events! The apostles had seen the miracles Jesus had done, and they witnessed also to his supernatural power and influence; they had seen his glory both at the crucifixion and at his resurrection from the dead. This was their unassailable tradition and this was the only truth that could be recognized as genuine. "No spirit is from God that denies that Jesus Christ did come in the flesh."

Within the churches there were widows who tended to become a burden on the other members. Sometimes their own grown-up children could have supported them, but had refused to do so. The churches had to help them, therefore. They were asked to assist the elders by visiting the sick

and consulting with women members in cases of moral
difficulty. In many congregations the younger widows were
advised to marry again, so that they would not be busy-
bodies, or easy prey for wandering teachers who begged
hospitality in the name of Jesus, and then turned out to be
rascals.

The moral standards of the Church had always to be protected; for there were conceited Christians like those at
Corinth in the days of Paul. Such people felt that they were
above all law; they became sensual and idle, they drank too
much wine, and their love affairs were scandalous. "Their
lives are directed by evil passions," wrote Jude. "They ko-
tow to the wealthy for their own advantage, but their
mouths are filled with loud talk. Such people are a menace
to the Love Feasts of the Church, they are utterly unstable,
they cause divisions, they are worldlings who are destitute
of the Holy Spirit of God."

Heresies of the mind and errors of the flesh were thus
a constant anxiety to the leaders of the churches. It was essential, in their opinion, that outsiders should not be able
to point the finger of scorn at Christians. If the Church was
weak, divided internally, undisciplined, and immoral, how
could it be in the pagan world of the Roman Empire a
visible expression of the Kingdom of God? How could it
be the one, true body of Christ in which his Spirit lived?
To escape divine judgment, the Church had to be loyal
to Jesus, loving and pure; it had no privileged position that
exempted it from obedience to the commandments. The
goodness and love of God ought never to be despised, for
the Lord Jesus had endured agony, humiliation, and the
awful loneliness of the cross that the Church might become
a reality.

Moreover, it was imperative that the churches should
preserve harmony within their own borders, for they were

about to face the gravest threat to their existence. The power of the Kingdom of God, as it expressed itself in the life of Christians, was about to be challenged by the might of the Caesars.

Titus, the conqueror of Jerusalem, had succeeded Vespasian on the throne of the Empire; and he in turn was followed by his brother Domitian. Shortly after the accession of Domitian, Rome was shocked by a report that Titus Flavius Clemens, the emperor's cousin, had been put to death by order of Domitian. Clemens had recently been consul, a colleague of the emperor during his term of office. The only charge against him, apparently, was a refusal to perform all the duties of the consulship. The report was genuine, and another of official rank, Aulus Glabrio, also was murdered. Domitilla, the wife of Clemens and niece of Domitian, was sent into exile. Fearing a new reign of terror, senators trembled in their shoes, and noble ladies, as they were carried up the narrow lanes of Rome in slave-drawn litters, lay closely hidden to escape detection. "What could the error of Domitilla and her husband have been?" they whispered to one another; and the best answer they received was that these aristocrats had been converted to "Jewish religious practices."

To become a Jew in religion would certainly mean a clash with the emperor. How could a consul who professed the Jewish faith in one God offer the sacrifices to Roman gods and goddesses? There had developed during the past century a custom of regarding the dead emperors as gods, and this was even more embarrassing. In Asia Minor and the East both the city of Rome and the emperor of Rome were deified, and the Asiatics did not wait until the rulers were dead. Now Domitian was demanding that in Rome too he should be hailed in his lifetime as "Lord and God."

Such claims Jews and Christians could never accept. Native-born Jews could seek the protection of the laws and treaties that safeguarded their right to observe their national religion; but these did not apply to Romans who had become converts to Judaism, nor to Christians of any nationality.

Faced by the demands of the State for religious homage to the emperor and by the threat of death as traitors if they refused, some members of the Church counseled compromise and the avoidance of open conflict. But was civil obedience the right course, or the only course? Had the Kingdom of God come with power after all, if the servants of the King submitted tamely to such idolatry?

There were Christians in the eastern provinces who said, "No!"

This devotion to Rome and its divine ruler had started in the city of Pergamum in Asia Minor. Here the magistrates insisted that throwing a few grains of incense on the altar dedicated to emperor worship was merely a sign of good citizenship, and not properly a religious act. Christians could and ought to conform like everyone else. Otherwise the authorities would rightly conclude that Christians were guilty of un-Roman activities. Tales were already current about these strange, unsociable folk with no visible god; at their Love Feasts, it was said, they ate the flesh and drank the blood of their Savior.

"I deny it all!" cried Antipas, a leader of the local church. To the Christians in Pergamum he said:

"Think what it means to admit publicly that Domitian is 'Lord.' When we became Christians, weren't we told that we had to renounce our pagan gods and goddesses in order to serve the one true and living God? We accepted that. We believed that Jesus Christ, the Son of God, gave his life once and for all for the sins of the world, and we confessed before the elders and the congregation, 'Jesus is Lord.' How many Lords can a man be expected to serve? If we call Domitian 'Lord,' doesn't that mean, and doesn't he intend us to mean, that we acknowledge him as a divinity? For that is certainly what we mean when we give this title to our Savior Christ. This is no matter of words: this means life or death for the Church! This is not hairsplitting, but holding fast to our traditions and our profession. For the whole basis of our religion is that in spirit we worship the Father through the Son, who became man for us men and for our salvation in the Kingdom of God. As I hope for eternal life in that Kingdom, I for one will not bow the knee to Domitian nor call him 'Lord'! I will never consent to offer a sacrifice at his altar. Jesus alone is our Lord, and by his grace we are the heirs of God's Kingdom."

For this stanch witness to the faith Antipas paid with his life. The Christians of Pergamum called the altar of Rome and the emperor "the throne of Satan."

Some other centers felt the impact of the imperial policy, and mobs shouted for the full penalties of the law on those who would not conform. Many died bravely, but many also tried to evade the issue or gave in. At Sardis, for example, far too large a number of Christians purchased immunity and escaped martyrdom by tossing the incense over the altar.

One leader of resolute spirit was the prophet and seer called John, who knew this record and did not hesitate to tell the churches of Asia Minor what he thought of them. His letters to them, and the account of the visions he had while an exile, were collected into a book that came to be called "The Revelation of John."

Ephesus had done fairly well, for its leaders had dealt effectively with false teachers there some ten years before; yet even Ephesus fell short in respect to Christian charity and sacrificial love. As for Sardis, it was spiritually dead!

"You have the reputation of being alive, but you are dead."
Philadelphia, although weak in numbers and influence,
was alive: "There is an open door set before you, and no
man can shut it. This is the voice of the Spirit; he who has
an ear, let him hear!"

For one church John reserved the worst condemnation:
"I was commanded to write to the 'angel' of the church in
Laodicea: 'The words of the Amen, the first of God's creation, a faithful and genuine witness. I know your works:
you are neither cold nor hot. I wish you were the one thing
or the other! Those whom I love I rebuke and discipline;
therefore acquire new zeal and change your ways. Behold,
I am standing at your door and knocking; if anyone hears
my voice and opens the door, I will come in to him and will
sup with him, and he will sup with me. To him that con-
quers I will grant to sit beside me on my throne, even as
I conquered and sat down beside my Father on his throne.
He who has an ear, let him hear what the Spirit is saying
to the churches.'"

It was inevitable that one who spoke so uncompromis-
ingly about the Church's duty to resist should be arrested
by the civil authorities. But John was fortunate; instead
of being martyred for the faith, he was exiled to the tiny
island of Patmos in the Aegean, west of Miletus.

As he brooded over the fate of the Church throughout
the Roman Empire in the face of the divine pretensions and
ungodly power of her government, John had wonderful
visions of God's glory, of the catastrophes that must fall
upon the earth if the will of God were flouted, and of the
splendors that awaited all who gave faithful testimony to
Jesus as Lord. Rome became for him the Antichrist, the
embodiment of all evil, the supreme enemy of Christ and
his people. Rome was a wicked fiend who sat in worldly
pride and magnificence on her seven hills, gloating over

the martyrs and plotting fresh terrors. She would do better
to think about her own folly and her perverse corruption!
What good were all her lovely temples and her fine palaces
if the men and women who were her citizens behaved like
beasts? Along the straight highways that brought everything
to Rome from the farthest corners of the Empire sped
vicious ideas and the satanic refinements of men grown mad
with power. Better for her if she remembered another imperial "god" who had set her on fire thirty years before
for a whim!

"Alas, alas, for the great city
that was clothed in fine linen, in purple and scarlet,
bedecked with gold, with jewels, and pearls!
In one hour all your wealth has been laid waste."
If it had happened already at such hands, how much more
and how much worse would be its fate in the Day when the
living God executed his vengeance!

In these visions John felt himself carried off in spirit to
the presence of the Almighty. On his throne in the courts of
heaven sat the Ancient of Days, the Lord God Omnipotent.
His appearance was brilliant, like jasper and agate. Above
the throne shone the rainbow, the symbol of the promise
made to Noah that the Lord would show mercy to mankind.
In a semicircle about the throne were placed twenty-four
bishops, the "angels" of the churches; they were clothed in
white robes and wore golden crowns. Everlasting fire
burned before the throne; lightning and thunder echoed
and re-echoed; the sound of many waters was heard. In that
divine court the heavenly hosts prostrated themselves continually in adoration:

"Holy, holy, holy, is the Lord God Omnipotent,
who was and is and is to come! . . .

"Worthy art thou, our Lord and God,
to receive glory and honor and power,
for thou didst create all things,
and by thy will they came to be and were created."

Nevertheless, the court of Domitian, the earthly pretender to divine glory, remained untouched by blasts from heaven. The great and dreadful Day of the Lord did not come. Christ, the lamb of God and the agent of God's wrath (as John believed), did not return on the clouds of the sky with his terrible sword in his right hand. The inhabitants of the Empire went their daily way as before, seeking fame, riches, and security; fearful of a future none could foretell and a death from which no one came back. Faithful Christians in the Empire seemed to their pagan neighbors an extraordinary people, who wanted nothing to do with wealth or with sensual pleasures. Christians tried by divine grace to love their enemies and to be merciful to all in distress. They were witnesses in a world of sorrow and fear to the patient purposes of a God who had made men for himself, but would rule them only in love. Jesus, whom Jews and Romans had put to death, was conqueror because he had consented to die in obedience to God and in love for his enemies. The cross was good news, but it was also a judgment on the self-seeking, the arrogant, and the unloving. Men must choose, therefore, between Christ and Caesar; between the kind of world Rome in its outward pomp represented and the kind of world God in Christ intended and was resolved to have.

John, the seer and prophet, saw the issues clearly, and was convinced that he had been called by the Spirit of Christ to sound a grave warning to the Church. He was to tell men about the end of all things and the Last Judgment. For God, he believed, might at any moment decide to bring the Roman world to the destruction it deserved, and with it make a final end of the kingdom of Satan.

His fellow Christians must be aroused to see how easy, how fatally easy, it was to yield to the powers of this world in order to be comfortable. He must awaken them to further perseverance and renewed courage. He must open their eyes to see that God in heaven was arrayed in all his majesty for war against Satan, and that the celestial hosts must surely triumph. As surely would the faithful on earth share God's victory! Into the wine press of the wrath of God would be poured the arrogance, the greed, and the idolatry of Rome and its pseudogod. Soon, soon the sickle would be put in, because the grapes of the vine that was on earth were ripe. God was the living and eternal God, and John was his chosen prophet and seer. To John the Spirit had revealed that God would never suffer evil to hold undisputed sway in his world. The kingdoms of this world were all to become the Kingdom of God and his Christ. But if God meant this, then God was at work and God would accomplish his purpose soon ... soon! His Christ would come and reign for a thousand years; then Satan and his hosts would be released for a short period till at last the end came.

John wrote down a record of his visions and required that it should be read by the understanding Christian; and the churches gave it heed and preserved it, even though the end seemed to linger and no Christ appeared to do battle against the evil forces of this world. From John they learned their high duty and dignity: "Jesus has made us a kingdom, priests to his God and Father; to him is the glory and dominion forever!" From John they received a vision of a new city, a Holy City. It was to be paradise regained, where men and women from every kindred and tribe and language would come to dwell together with God and with one another, bringing all their treasures to lay them before the throne of God and the Lamb that had been slain. The name of this heavenly city was "the new Jerusalem." It needed no Temple, since God was ever present and accessible to his worshipers. It was to have no sun and no moon; for in this place there would be eternal day, and Jesus their Lord was the light of their world forever. Flowing from beneath the throne of God would be the river of the water of life, and upon its banks would grow the tree of life, which bore a different fruit for each month of the year: "And the leaves of the tree are for the healing of the nations." Thus there could be no more death there and no sorrow, for God "will wipe away all tears from their eyes." In that city the Church, which is the body and bride of Christ, would sit down to the marriage feast of the Lamb, and there would be joy and happiness for all the redeemed. The beloved of God would sing the song of Moses and of the Lamb:

"Great and wonderful are thy deeds,
O Lord God the Omnipotent!
Just and true are thy ways,
O King of the nations!
Who shall not fear and glorify thy name, O Lord?
For thou only art holy.
All nations shall come and worship thee,
For thy judgments have been revealed."

Thus John, and the churches that treasured the story of his indomitable faith, maintained the conviction that one day all the ends of the earth would come to adore and lovingly serve, in spirit and in truth, the Heavenly Father who had been revealed in Jesus Christ. From the gates of the Atlantic to the shores of Palestine; on both coasts of the Mediterranean; in North Africa, Italy, and Greece; far up the island-studded shore of Asia Minor to distant Pontus and beyond, to the borders of the steppes where the dreaded

Scythians lived; across the Syrian deserts and in the cities of the Roman world, the message of the love of God was traveling and conquering; and upon those who waited patiently for the final triumph of the Kingdom fell the benedictions of John of Patmos:

"The Spirit and the Bride say, 'Come'; and let him who hears say, 'Come.' . . . He who bears witness to these things says, 'Surely I am coming soon.' Amen. Come, Lord Jesus! The grace of the Lord Jesus be with all the saints. . . .

"The kingdom of the world has become the kingdom of our Lord and of his Christ, and he shall reign forever and ever! . . .

"Hallelujah! For the Lord God Omnipotent is reigning!"

SCRIPTURE REFERENCES